TEACHING ACTING WITH PRACTICAL AESTHETICS

Teaching Acting with Practical Aesthetics uses constructivist pedagogy to teach acting via Practical Aesthetics, a system of actor training created in the mid-1980s by David Mamet.

The book melds the history of Practical Aesthetics, Practical Aesthetics itself, educational theory, and compatible physical work into the educational approach called Praxis to create a comprehensive training guide for the modern actor and theatre instructor. It includes lesson plans, compatible voice and movement exercises, constructivist teaching materials, classroom handouts, and a suggested calendar for acting courses.

Written for Acting instructors at the college and secondary levels, Acting scholars, and professionals looking for a new way to perform, *Teaching Acting with Practical Aesthetics* offers detailed instructions to help students sharpen their performing skills and excel on stage.

Troy L. Dobosiewicz, PhD is an Assistant Professor of Theatre at Ball State University in Muncie, IN. He teaches courses in Theatre Education, Acting, Theatre History, and Introduction to Theatre.

TEACHING ACTING WITH PRACTICAL AESTHETICS

Troy L. Dobosiewicz

NEW YORK AND LONDON

First published 2020
by Routledge
52 Vanderbilt Avenue, New York, NY 10017

and by Routledge
2 Park Square, Milton Park, Abingdon, Oxon OX14 4RN

Routledge is an imprint of the Taylor & Francis Group, an informa business

© 2020 Taylor & Francis

The right of Troy L. Dobosiewicz to be identified as author of this work has been asserted by him in accordance with sections 77 and 78 of the Copyright, Designs and Patents Act 1988.

All rights reserved. No part of this book may be reprinted or reproduced or utilised in any form or by any electronic, mechanical, or other means, now known or hereafter invented, including photocopying and recording, or in any information storage or retrieval system, without permission in writing from the publishers.

Trademark notice: Product or corporate names may be trademarks or registered trademarks, and are used only for identification and explanation without intent to infringe.

Library of Congress Cataloging-in-Publication Data
Names: Dobosiewicz, Troy L., author.
Title: Teaching acting with practical aesthetics / Troy L. Dobosiewicz.
Description: New York, NY : Routledge, 2020. | Includes bibliographical references and index.
Identifiers: LCCN 2019016033| ISBN 9780367231095 (hardback : alk. paper) | ISBN 9780367231118 (pbk. : alk. paper) | ISBN 9780429290688 (ebook)
Subjects: LCSH: Acting--Study and teaching. | Aesthetics--Study and teaching. | Constructivism (Education)
Classification: LCC PN2075 .D63 2020 | DDC 792.02/807--dc23
LC record available at https://lccn.loc.gov/2019016033

ISBN: 978-0-367-23109-5 (hbk)
ISBN: 978-0-367-23111-8 (pbk)
ISBN: 978-0-429-29068-8 (ebk)

Typeset in Bembo
by Taylor & Francis Books

To Mrs. Barbara Farrelly, James McNab, and Jeanette Ciesielski . . . your perseverance taught me more than you ever imagined.

CONTENTS

List of tables		*viii*
Acknowledgements		*ix*

Introduction: Teaching acting using Practical Aesthetics		1
1	Examining Practical Aesthetics	6
2	Constructivism	21
3	Teaching acting using Constructivist Learning Design	29
4	Praxis is theory in action	38
5	Training the mind to use Practical Aesthetics	45
6	Training the voice while using Practical Aesthetics	87
7	Training the body while using Practical Aesthetics	107
8	Closure	127

Appendix	*135*
Index	*144*

TABLES

5.1	"First Day of Class: Introductions"	48
5.2	"Mind, Voice, Body and Level I Repetition"	52
5.3	"Level I, II, and III Repetition"	56
5.4	"Practical Aesthetics Scene Analysis"	63
5.5	"Analyzing Assigned Scenes"	67
5.6	"Playing the 'As if Game'"	73
5.7	"Using Tools"	78
5.8	"Shifting Tools"	82
5.9	"Rehearsal into Performance"	86
6.1	"Warming Up the Vocal Instrument"	97
6.2	"Examining Breath, Resonance, and Pitch"	101
6.3	"Articulation and Tongue Twisters"	105
7.1	"Breathing, Stretching, and Strengthening"	113
7.2	"Presence, Laban Kinesphere, and Ensemble"	120
7.3	"Improvisation for Movement"	125

ACKNOWLEDGEMENTS

I want to express my gratitude to Routledge's editorial staff. Their guidance and help made it manageable for me to complete this book. I am so thankful for their quick and professional responses to all my questions during the publication process. I also wish to express my thanks to Ball State University's Department of Theatre and Dance. Your kind words of congratulations, keep going, and class scheduling made it possible for me to write this book. Lastly, I want to thank all my teachers from grade eight to the present. Your academic support made nothing seem impossible. When you read this book, you will notice that it was written for Theatre Educators who are in the field or will be entering the field. It is my way of giving back to you what you gave me. Please use what I have gathered to enhance your current classroom methodologies and to prepare the next generation of Theatre Educators for any academic level of instruction.

INTRODUCTION

Teaching acting using Practical Aesthetics

In the mid-1990s, I began my career as a collegiate and secondary theatre instructor. I had just finished my master's degree in theatre and felt I was ready to take on the responsibilities of both positions. I quickly realized, as I would guess all theatre generalists eventually do, that I was better at some parts of these jobs than others. Over the following years I worked to hone my skills in all areas of theatre instruction and production. The one area that provided the greatest challenge came from the students in my introductory acting classes. I am not talking about learning how to direct them via line readings or showing them where to stand; I am talking about really and truly guiding them to the point of becoming living, thinking, breathing, and reacting actors. I could run them through various learning activities and do every sort of standard character analysis, but what I saw in the classroom rarely transferred to the stage.

It was a distressing realization. I purchased book after book and attended meetings and conferences across the United States in hopes of finding out the secret to unlocking and developing the novice actor. In fact, my greatest hope was built on a single session led by famous adult and child acting teacher Bella Itkin. The session, which was held in the late 1990s at an Association for Theatre in Higher Education (ATHE) Conference, was called something generic like "How to Teach Acting." I arrived early and sat with great anticipation as Itkin began the session. She said, "I have been teaching the 'unteachable' subject of acting for forty years." I sat there in shock; I was absolutely devastated. Itkin described several techniques but provided no complete answer. She did not use a system I could duplicate because her success was located within Bella Itkin herself. This "guru system" of acting instruction is effective, so the term is not pejorative. There just seems to be something special in individual acting instructors that resonates with acting students. I wondered if I needed to find that in myself.

My analytic mind eventually doubted this consideration. I just could not accept that only "acting gurus" can teach acting. I also did not believe that the key to an actor's success is some amorphous characteristic we call talent. Accidentally pairing a talented actor with a guru instructor cannot be the only road to success. No. It seemed more probable to me that an acting guru actually has a system; they just do not know how to articulate it or record it on paper. Current popular acting text books did not provide the answer either. In addition, my ability to act was irrelevant to most of my students. I actually considered a career change because I was so frustrated.

In 2000, I decided to do a summer-long intensive in New York City to see if I should use my talent and simply become an actor. A friend of mine, who spent years performing on Broadway and is now chair of a university theatre department, suggested I investigate the Atlantic Theatre Acting School. She did not know a great deal about its program, but she heard that the faculty seemed to be interested in the systematic teaching of acting. Atlantic's system of actor training, called *Practical Aesthetics*, was developed by David Mamet, William H. Macy, and a select number of Mamet's students from Goddard College in Vermont. I enrolled in the school.

My goal was to become a professional actor who uses the system, but something else happened because my instructors kept repeating the phrase: "Practical Aesthetics is easier to learn if you have never performed, or if you have never taken any acting classes." The teacher in me started thinking, "I'll bet my novice college and secondary school actors could learn this Practical Aesthetics system rather quickly. They would then have at their fingertips one concise, reliable, and systematic way of preparing a role and executing the performance of that role." My students at that time could complete classroom and rehearsal hall acting exercises, but they often failed to use what they learned from those exercises when they stepped on stage. This type of transfer is a major problem with novice actors. They can master theatre games, skillfully perform improvisations, and write novel-length character analyses offstage, but that work fades from memory when they step on stage. I decided to keep two sets of notes during my Practical Aesthetics training at the Atlantic to address my current dilemmas: one set was for Troy Dobosiewicz, the professional actor trying to improve his acting abilities, and the other set was for Troy Dobosiewicz the collegiate and secondary school acting instructor who would need to teach Practical Aesthetics.

I found myself grappling more with how to teach the system than how to use the system. It was fascinating to me. Therefore, this book is for theatre educators: students training to be theatre teachers, instructors teaching at the college level, and/or those teaching acting workshops. I kept track of the methods that seemed to work, modified others because I was familiar with young adults, and dismissed those not useful to the student in me. I then returned to my teaching positions in Northern Virginia where the call to teach was too strong. I decided to remain a full-time teacher instead of becoming a professional actor, but I instituted Practical Aesthetics at the places where I taught.

Since the fall of 2000, I have taught my modified system of Practical Aesthetics to students in Northern Virginia, Northern Indiana, and New York City. This system of actor training is unlike anything else I have experienced. Practical Aesthetics allows my students to excel as actors because classroom training easily transfers to the stage. My students also felt the difference and were amazed by their new-found abilities. Ironically, I had no idea what was operating within Practical Aesthetics that led to this success; I just knew it worked.

After teaching for a bit, I decided to earn my PhD in theatre. I wanted to truly influence future theatre artists and even future theatre instructors and actors. While doing so I realized something. It was not just Practical Aesthetics that was leading to my success. I was using a teaching style in my classes that complemented Practical Aesthetics. I was utilizing a *Constructivist* approach to the teaching of acting. Pairing that approach with Practical Aesthetics was seamless and natural. I was using a completely different approach to teaching acting that did not fit in with the "banking model of education" so often used in our academic institutions today,

The "banking model of education," a phrase coined by Paulo Freire in his landmark text *Pedagogy of the Oppressed*, is defined as follows:

> Instead of communicating, the teacher issues communiques and makes deposits which the students patiently receive, memorize, and repeat ... In the banking concept of education, knowledge is a gift bestowed by those who consider themselves knowledgeable upon those whom they consider to know nothing. Projecting an absolute ignorance onto others, a characteristic of the ideology of oppression, negates education and knowledge as processes of inquiry. The teacher presents himself to his students as their necessary opposite; by considering their ignorance absolute, he justifies his own existence. The students, alienated like the slave in the Hegelian dialectic, accept their ignorance as justifying the teacher's existence – but, unlike the slave, they never discover that they educate the teacher. (58–59)

Constructivism is diametrically opposed to the banking model of education. At its very heart, it requires the instructor and students to practice a give and take in the classroom. It is dialogue, not didacticism that also makes Practical Aesthetics a valuable method of instruction – especially now when our schools need instructors who can teach critical thinking and not simply rote memorization. I did not force a constructivist approach onto the content of Practical Aesthetics; my pedagogy fit the system. In fact, only after a few years as a doctoral student at Arizona State University and in my fifth year as Assistant Professor of Theatre at Ball State University did I discover I was a progressive educator. I simply had a problem and found a creative solution by joining constructivist pedagogy with

Practical Aesthetics. I knew a book on acting for future theatre educators at the secondary and collegiate level would be the next step in my career.

Unlike the few books available that discuss Practical Aesthetics, this book is not pure description, nor is it just for the actor to apply to his/her own work. This is a handbook for the instructor who has been searching for the same things I have, for the secondary and college instructor who simply wishes to try something different in the classroom, for the scholar interested in constructivist education and/or the art of acting, and even for the actor who wishes to understand Practical Aesthetics in greater detail. I constantly learn, add, and adapt my methods, but I hope I have presented a theoretically sound system of actor education that can "turn on that little light bulb" instructors always look for hovering over our students' heads. In addition, I believe actors themselves can learn a great deal about the system that other texts simply do not provide. Because of this approach, this book can be thought of as a presentation of *Theory* and practice transformed into *Praxis*. Theory propels my teaching and practice into *Praxis*, the melding of theory and practice to create a detailed system for training novice actors and helping instructors teach acting.

The first, second, and third chapters can be thought of as the *Theory* portion of this book. In Chapter 1, I introduce Practical Aesthetics as an acting system by defining the system, offering a review of the literature currently available about Practical Aesthetics, and providing a descriptive analysis of the system itself. In Chapter 2, I discuss constructivism as both an epistemology and pedagogy. I also provide a review of the literature on constructivism and describe the theory itself. In Chapter 3, I examine Constructivist Learning Design. In Chapter 4, I apply both theory and practice to introduce the concept of *Praxis* as it pertains to teaching Practical Aesthetics.

The actual *Praxis* portions of this book focus on using constructivist methods and Practical Aesthetics to train the three tools of the actor: mind, voice, and body. Chapter 5 is titled "Training the mind to use Practical Aesthetics," Chapter 6 is titled "Training the voice while using Practical Aesthetics," and Chapter 7 covers "Training the body while using Practical Aesthetics." The praxis-based lessons are first presented as narratives, but each includes a constructivist analysis of the lesson itself. I have chosen this approach so instructors can both theoretically and practically understand the lessons. This also makes it possible for the lessons to be utilized immediately in the classroom.

The last chapter of this book is titled Chapter 8 "Closure" and contains my concluding remarks. The "Closure" is followed by an Appendix that contains a suggested course calendar for an acting class, constructivist teaching materials, and classroom handouts which include a performance rubric. These can be reproduced and used in the classroom. Of course, it is possible to skip directly to the *Praxis* section and implement Practical Aesthetics immediately, but I suggest reading the entire book. Instructors can then utilize constructivism to frame their approach to teaching theatre while also developing new constructivist acting exercises as they see how the material progresses.

I contend that constructivism and Practical Aesthetics lend themselves well to fashioning an actor training system for beginning actors. When implemented using constructivist pedagogy, Practical Aesthetics allows instructors to create an integrated acting program, not a program made up of fragmented exercises that students often do not know how to integrate themselves. In addition, actors can transition from the rehearsal hall to the stage seamlessly due to Practical Aesthetics' transparent building block process. This is what is missing from the field—clear building blocks.

There are many acting instructors who are great actors, but they still have difficulty teaching others to do what they do on stage. Similarly, there are too many students who cannot fully understand why they are doing the acting exercises found in several popular text books on acting. I write this book to help with these problems. I attempt to put a clear, concise, and further distilled acting system, revealed through the pedagogical methods constructivism brings to light, into the hands of those who wish to use it.

Reference

Freire, Paulo, Myra B. Ramos, Donaldo P. Macedo, and Ira Shor. *Pedagogy of the Oppressed*. New York: Bloomsbury Academic. 2018. Print.

1

EXAMINING PRACTICAL AESTHETICS

In the early 1980s, David Mamet and several of his theatre students from Goddard College in Vermont wanted to develop a distinct system to train actors. Mamet wanted a trustworthy training system that could easily be learned and applied (Bruder, *Practical Handbook* x–xi). The system also needed to provide a clear and concise way to approach acting and directing. "Grounded philosophically in the tenets of the Greek philosopher Epictetus and psychologically in the theories of William James, Mamet developed what he later called Practical Aesthetics" (Atlantic Theatre Company). This book includes explanations and downloadable worksheet material that instructors should read to the point of habituation that guide them through the process. This book is about teaching the system for those training to be Theatre Education majors at any level, college acting instructors, and actors wishing to widen their methodological repertoire. The *Oxford English Dictionary* (*OED*) defines *practical* as "relating to practice or action, as opposed to speculation or theory ... designating that area of a particular subject or discipline in which ideas or theories are tested or applied in practice." The *OED* defines *aesthetics* as "the distinctive underlying principles of a work of art or a genre" (oed.com). Therefore, Practical Aesthetics is an appropriate name for the system since it calls for the methodical active application of a set of strategies by an actor to create and perform a role during the art of rehearsal and theatrical performance. Practical Aesthetics can provide a kind of "road map" for the actor from rehearsal to performance. By following its guidelines, the system develops the skills of each actor at an individual level and pace so that an individual can create truthful moments on stage.

There are very few sources that decode the Practical Aesthetics system. What seems to be the most compact description is an online article called *Practical Aesthetics—An Overview* by Mark Westbrook (ezinarticles.com). This is a basic description, but makes the mistake of saying "learning Practical Aesthetics is easy," a point of view that does not value the discipline and practice demanded for successful application of this technique (ezinarticles.com). Similarly, another basic source on Practical Aesthetics is the chapter on David Mamet found in Richard Brestoff's *The Great Acting Teachers and Their Methods*, Vol. 2. Brestoff provides a limited biography about Mamet and writes about Practical Aesthetics as if the reader was an actor in a class at the Atlantic Theatre Acting School. This approach allows the reader to get a taste of what it might be like to be in the classroom, but it does not facilitate a comprehensive analysis and documentation of the system.

The most detailed source on Practical Aesthetics is Melissa Bruder, et al.'s *A Practical Handbook for the Actor*, which has not been updated since its original publication in 1986. That is problematic because changes have been made to the Practical Aesthetics system since that time. In addition, Bruder's text is written by an actor for an actor. The book attempts to teach the reader the system. As a novice, however, I did not fully understand the book until after I trained at the Atlantic Theatre Acting School in New York. That is problematic for the actor and the Theatre Educator who are unable to train at the Atlantic or one of its subsidiaries.

Two sources, limited in scope and depth, are available for anyone interested in learning the basics of the Practical Aesthetics system: *Training of the American Actor* and *Handbook of Acting Techniques*, both edited by Arthur Bartow. Bartow was the artistic director of the drama department at NYU's Tisch School of the Arts. Interestingly, except for a new introductory section, the books are the same; one was published in the United States and the second was published in the UK. I was pleased to learn, however, that the chapter in each book devoted to Practical Aesthetics, "Practical Aesthetics: An Overview," was written by Robert Bella, my instructor at the Atlantic Theatre Acting School. He does an excellent job providing a full description of the system, but it is not enough to truly put it into practice or teach it to others. Bella's chapter is missing a method of instruction. In fact, that is the main reason I am writing this book. This text can be used by Theatre Educators in the classroom and by students interested in learning more about this technique.

There is a final book that examines the system differently. *Theatre as Life: Practical Wisdom Drawn from Great Acting Teachers, Actors, & Actresses* by Paul Marcus and his daughter Gabriela Marcus, talks about using acting techniques in everyday life. Paul Marcus is a psychologist and Gabriela Marcus is an actress. Essentially a self-help book, the authors devote several pages to critiquing David Mamet as a person before suggesting that Practical Aesthetics can be useful to the everyday person living his/her everyday life. Their application is not the focus of my work; I am interested in Practical Aesthetics for the theatre. I also believe the best way to do this is to invoke constructivist pedagogy. That is why this text melds theory, process, practice, and a teaching and learning epistemology (or ways of knowing) to make Practical Aesthetics available to actors and students.

Currently, Practical Aesthetics is taught at the Atlantic Theatre Acting School which is part of the Atlantic Theatre, founded by David Mamet and William H. Macy in 1985. Theatre artists can train directly through the Atlantic Theatre Acting School or through a partnership between the Atlantic Theatre and New York University's Tisch School of the Arts. In addition, the Atlantic Theatre Acting School operates a branch in Los Angeles and another in Sydney, Australia. The existence of three branches of the Atlantic and its partnership with New York University speaks to the presence of Practical Aesthetics in today's theatrical world.

In a letter dated July 21, 1985, David Mamet wrote the Atlantic Theatre Acting Company and said, "Our company is founded not on talent, not on effect, but on discipline" (Personal Letter). Interestingly, the discipline he is referring to is the discipline espoused by the Stoic philosopher Epictetus in his *Enchiridion*. The text states, "Some things are in our control and others not. Things in our control are opinion, pursuit, desire, aversion, and, in a word, whatever are our own actions. Things not in our control are body, property, reputation, command, and, in one word, whatever are not our own actions" (1). Pursuit and desire could be interpreted as keywords for Mamet. Interpreting Epictetus, it is only possible to master Practical Aesthetics if one has the desire to pursue mastery through discipline. Epictetus continues:

> If you see an attractive person, you will find that self-restraint is the ability you have against your desire. If you are in pain, you will find fortitude. If you hear unpleasant language, you will find patience. And thus habituated, the appearances of things will not hurry you away along with them. (10)

Essentially, discipline can force an individual to develop habits that make it possible to face and overcome obstacles. If acting can be framed as continually overcoming obstacles, then actors must develop disciplined habits to perform effectively. The Practical Aesthetics system provides a system to develop these disciplined habits. But success on stage is then only possible via personally understanding and habitually using the system. As a professor of Theatre Education, who teaches future teachers how to teach acting, and as an acting instructor I contend that constructivist pedagogy makes this possible and provides a match to the system. I will expound on this pedagogy later in the book, and why it is a method of teaching and learning Practical Aesthetics.

Mamet also relies heavily on chapter IV, "Habit," from William James' *Principles of Psychology*. James believes habit to be a result of education via repetition and discipline (108). "Thus we notice after exercising our muscles or our brain in a new way, that we can do so no longer at that time; but after a day or two of rest, when we resume the discipline, our increase in skill not seldom surprises us" (110). James also believes that when learned, a habit changes the brain physiologically (109). "The most complex habits ... are ... nothing but concatenated discharges in the nerve-centers, due to the presence there of systems of reflex paths, so organized as to wake each other up successively" (108). A fascinating theoretical explanation, given the complete absence of computer technology at the time. By combining the theories of James and Epictetus, Mamet believes the disciplined learning and habituation of Practical Aesthetics can be the key to becoming a good actor. As I have said before, what is missing is a pedagogical methodology: constructivism. To begin, however, I will explain the elements of Practical Aesthetics: Repetition and Scene Analysis.

Repetition

The first part of the Practical Aesthetics method begins with what I have named Level I, Level II, and Level III Repetition. Although the basic concept of "repetition" was borrowed from Sanford Meisner and is part of Practical Aesthetics, what follows is my interpretation and personal modification for the teaching of Mamet's Repetition exercises (Lahr 70). Remember Edward James' notion of habituation? James believed habit to be a result of education via repetition and discipline (108). Without these eventually habituated distinctions (which must be clearly made by using verbal, aural, and kinesthetic methods) I have found it nearly impossible to help actors realize the most basic tenants of Practical Aesthetics. I have witnessed many instructors completely fail a group of beginning actors in this early stage, because habituation requires time and patience. It is not something mastered in a day; it is complex. For example, in his book *The Sanford Meisner Approach*, Larry Silverberg attempts to deal with repetition. I find his interpretation too personally digested, as I do Meisner's approach. It is as if both need to be present to lead the exercises. I mean no offense, but the "guru approach" is not what my interpretation of Practical Aesthetics espouses. That is why this book includes explanations which instructors should read to the point of habituation and downloadable worksheet material for student actors to guide them through the process. This book is about teaching.

In Level I Repetition, actors are placed in pairs, told to focus on one another, and say the first thing they see. The key, as with improvisation, is the performer may not disagree or say "no." The reason is whether an individual believes something to be true about himself/herself does not mean others agree. Others may see something completely different. Now, chance determines who makes the first observation, but in Level I the performers can only say the first thing they see about the other performer's physical body. It cannot be mean or meant to break up the exercise, and vocal intonation is completely ignored in Level I Repetition. Comical, swooping, or strange voices are actually hurtful to the exercise. What they show is an actor's unwillingness to engage with his/her partner. In addition, the statement must take the form: "You have …" "you are wearing …" "your hair is …" etc. It is also of utmost importance that the performers only say the first thing they notice about the other actor in that moment. For example, one performer might say, "You have brown eyes." If the other performer does not notice something about his/her partner's physical body, he/she must repeat what the first performer said; however, it must be repeated in the form: "I have ..." "I am wearing ..." "My hair is ..." etc. Therefore, he/she would respond, "I have brown eyes." The first performer would then repeat "You have brown eyes." This may create a loop of repeating the same observation; however, repeating the same observation is completely acceptable at this point. They are just learning. Therefore, the second performer may repeat, "I have brown eyes" or state a new physical observation about the first performer. The performers need to learn how to notice new things, but repeating is acceptable until they are capable of doing this. The main purpose of the exercise is to allow the partners to use observation to make personal connections with one another, something all actors strive to do. This process can continue for as long as the performers or instructor wish. In class, if the actors are adept at this process, the instructor will probably not need to guide them through it. If the actors are not adept, it is the job of the instructor to keep the performers focused on the exercise. Once the performers become adept at Level I Repetition, they move to Level II Repetition.

Level II Repetition requires the performers to look beyond the physical. Their observations may identify what appears to be a mental or emotional state, but vocal play should be at a minimum or not at all. Observations might include: "You look nervous," "You seem angry," "You are happy," etc. The repetition process follows the same process discussed in Level I. The performers may also include Level I observations, but they must strive to get to Level II to create deeper personal connections. If the actors are not adept at the process the instructor must keep the performers focused on the exercise. The instructor determines whether the performers have mastered Level II before they can move to Level III.

Level III Repetition is the most challenging level for the performers, because an active voice may finally be included. At Level III, performers must look beyond the physical, beyond the mental or emotional, and make a still deeper observation and connection. If we assume Level II Repetition requires the partners to identify emotional states, then Level III is asking the partners to identify the thought or thoughts behind those emotional states. Here the thoughts are revealed by the face, the body, and/or the voice. I realize "thoughts" is a vague term, so I believe examples are best used to create a solid understanding of how I am using the word. For instance, the "thoughts" identified might be, "You know exactly what you are doing right now," "You understand this completely," "You are angry at me," "You want to learn more," "You dislike this exercise," "You think you are better at this than I am," etc. Again, the instructor is the person who determines mastery of Level III Repetition which is the ability of an actor to look beyond the physical and interpret the emotional responses of his/her partner. When mastered, the process must be practiced. My instructors at the Atlantic Theatre Acting School suggested that we practice repetition for at least one hour per class day. If rehearsing for a performance, repetition should be done outside rehearsal time for one hour per day. The benefits for the beginning actor can be tremendous, because repetition encourages focus.

Yet, at this point a common response in my classroom is laughter. In our current society we look at phones rather than one another. So, staring at someone and identifying something may be comical. I indulge the laughter. Why not do so for a brief time? This will allow the students to get that impulse out of their systems. Then you can get back to actors focusing on one another. The instructor will sense the time needed to return to focus.

Since Mamet believes that an actor must focus on the other person or persons on stage instead of himself/herself, the purpose of repetition is to establish a connection via a point of focus (*True and False* 111). The process also makes actors comfortable being honest and working with one another. Once focused and comfortable, Mamet believes the scene will stay "in the moment" (111). The actor, because of repetition and their newly developed focus, will be able to notice any changes in a fellow actor during rehearsal and modify his/her performance to stay "in the moment" with the other actor. Every production will be different. Ideally the actors are not looking in their heads trying to remember lines. They will be actively engaged with one another. Although more about the value of constructivist pedagogy in these exercises will be covered later, a constructivist instructor helps build a schema or schemata that incorporate this engagement with one another. At this point, however, they have yet to touch a script or do scene analysis. That will follow. Actors using Practical Aesthetics must be open to learning a different technique. This will be something they never experienced before. If they start borrowing from other systems they know in an attempt to sneak through the system, the constructivist instructor must see that and say, "No, let's repeat again." For example, I always tell my students that words themselves are actually meaningless. Actors give words meaning by who says them, why they are said, when they are said, and most importantly HOW they are said. It is quite easy for an actor to mean "I hate you" while saying "I love you."

Scene analysis

After mastering Practical Aesthetics' Repetition, the next step is to read the play so scene analysis can begin. An actor must read the play being performed several times (even if he/she is in class and only has a scene that will be used for training). If in rehearsal for a full-length play, I prefer to do table work where we break the play into scenes and beats. Beats can always be modified if something changes in rehearsal. Nevertheless, the play, the scene, and each beat must be fully analyzed. For the purposes of this book, I will use a two-person scene as a unit of analysis. Instructors and directors may then use the same technique to analyze a play, a multi-character scene, or for individual beats within a scene.

Once a scene has been chosen for class performance, each performer memorizes it with no internal analysis. An actor should just have the words memorized. It defeats the purpose of Practical Aesthetics to walk into class already knowing how one is going to play a specific character in a specific scene. The reason is, an actor may walk out of class with a completely different analysis of the scene. It all comes down to what I mentioned in the repetition exercises: focusing on the other. I have found it extremely beneficial for scene partners to work on analysis together in class. Therefore, upon arrival and after some repetition exercises, scene partners sit down together with the downloadable worksheets or instructor handouts I provide in the Appendix of this book. The actors answer the questions provided in exact order knowing things may change in performance. At this point, the key is to determine what each character is literally doing in a scene, the character's wants, the character's action, and the actor's "as if"

What am I literally doing?

Determining what a character is literally doing is often more difficult than it sounds because performers tend to over-analyze. It is essential that the performers avoid interpretation at this level. The instructor must insist that they just look at the surface. The answer should be as simple as: "Two people meet for their first date," "A mother and daughter walk in their apartment at the same time, 3 am," or "Two brothers are discussing how much money they made today." They should not pry any deeper.

What do I want?

After the performers have determined what the characters are literally doing, the next step is to determine what each character wants. This step is actually missing from Melissa Bruder's text, *A Practical Handbook for the Actor*; however, the step is essential for clarity and must be supported by the text. The "want" should be each actor's personal decision, because the "want" must involve the other character in some way. Referencing the mock topics I already shared above, one cannot decide "I want to leave." Yet, one could say "I want to go to bed with this person immediately," or "I want be the one sneaking in at 3 am," or "I want to tell my brother what a great day I had today." Again, this must be supported by the text, and in this system an actor must focus on the other person not himself/herself. This distinction is important because it even has impact on the next level of analysis. The "want" must be clearly established before moving on to the next level of scene analysis.

What is my action?

Next, the performer must decide the character's "action." The term "action" is tricky and must be clearly defined according to Practical Aesthetics. "Action" does not mean simply doing something; it means "something that can be done."

The choice of actions can be tested against the following checklist of nine criteria:

1. It must be in line with the playwright's intentions.
2. It must not be an errand.
3. It must have a cap [what would this look like if I got it?].
4. It mustn't be emotionally or physically manipulative.
5. It mustn't predetermine an emotional state.
6. It must have its test in the other person [the action is applicable to the other character].
7. It must be specific.
8. It must be physically capable of being done.
9. It must be fun [to motivate each actor]. If the action changes, a new beat begins and a new analysis is performed. (Westbrook)

According to the aforementioned checklist, some examples of actions are "to get someone to take a chance," "to get what is owed me," "to show someone who is boss," "to get someone to 'wake up and smell the coffee,'" "to get someone to accept my special gift," or "to get someone to face the facts." Notice it is helpful to use the words "to get" or "to show" as prefixes to the actual "action." Providing this initial format allows the performer to get a better sense of what an "action" really is. Obviously the instructor can guide a performer toward a logical "action" if the performer seems lost. It is important to remember that any beat change in "want" can warrant a new "action." Therefore, the actors may have to play a series of "actions." This depends on the scene.

What is my "As if?"

Once the "action" is chosen, it is then the performer's task to determine his/her "as if." In Practical Aesthetics the "as if" literally provides a strand of connection to a life experience or a fantasy. In essence, the performer chooses a real-life situation or an imaginary situation where he or she tried "to get someone to take a chance," "to get what was owed him/her," "to show someone who is boss," etc. A real-life situation is helpful for student understanding, but they should never draw upon traumatic experiences. If the performer chooses to use an "as if" he/she imagines to have taken place or wishes to take place, it must be treated as an actual event would be. I always suggest that novice performers first learning the system use an actual event because that builds a personal understanding of that specific "action" within the actor. This link to constructivist pedagogy can facilitate the construction or modification of a mental plan/diagram, about the "action" being played when performing. But it is only a link. The actor is not reliving the actual event or even pulling the actual emotional feeling. For example, if the scene is about one's dog dying, the actor does not relive what it was like when his/her dog was dying. Nor does one think of his/her dying dog in a scene when his/her father is dying. Never. It's simply about knowing where to go with this new text. For clarification, the "as if" is meant to function like this: the actor playing a scene in which his/her dog died might think it unfair. Therefore, playing "to get someone to see things my way" loosely connected to an experience when the actor did not get his way as a child plants a seed of recognition, but avoids a possible emotionally dangerous reaction. The essence of the scene is still present, but not the gut-wrenching emotional recall that can cause psychological harm and possibly pull the actor out of the scene and/or work against the text. This protects the actor from getting lost in emotion while being true to the text. This makes the required "as if" present in Practical Aesthetics different from elements of other acting systems. This is also why the instructor must exercise caution. He/she should never try to get a performer to use extraordinarily painful events for the "as if." That is a trap that can traumatize. Instead, the actor should look for that seed from life, or use a fantasy as a seed of recognition to be true to the text instead of falling into an emotional quagmire. Theatre Educators working at the secondary level must be especially wary of this trap.

At this point, the instructor's role becomes even more essential. The instructor can identify whether the chosen "actions" and "as ifs" work or fit the scene. The "actions" have to work and they must be appropriate to the scene. The "as if" chosen by an actor should correlate to the intensity with which he/she pursues the "action." This can also be thought of as the importance of the "action." Therefore, if the intensity is either too high or too low, the instructor must intervene and question the "actions," "as if," and/or even the scene itself. The whole scene may have to be analyzed again, but the instructor works with the actors to discover effective choices. It is essential that the instructor does not tell the actors exactly what "action" to play. The actors must be able to construct their own personal "links" to the scene guided by the instructor.

After choosing the "action" and the "as if," it is time for the performers to interact without using the text. Mamet calls this exercise "playing 'the as if game'" (Westbrook). In the "as if game," the actors sit in a pair as though they were going to practice repetition. Instead of practicing repetition, the performers take seats facing each other and imagine themselves in their own "as if" situation. Each takes turns improvising their "as if" situation AT one another. They are to imagine that the other performer is the actual person in their "as if." They are not supposed to listen to one another. Instead, they base what they say in the improvisation on what they SEE in the other actor. Visual cues allow each actor to modify what they are saying. They can practice using different tactics based on the visuals to achieve what they want to achieve in their "as if" situation. This is practice for the stage, because it allows a performer to react to visual cues and body language rather than to text alone. The repetition exercises provide practice for this "as if" improvisation and now leads us to an examination of "tactics" mentioned before.

What are my tactics?

A performer gets his/her "action" by using a series of what are called "tactics" that lead to the attainment of the "action" (Westbrook). Based on what one performer sees in another, a "tactic" is used as a form of persuasion. Some obvious "tactics" might be flattery, bribery, anger, seduction, begging, bargaining, fear, etc.; however, "tactics" are not playing emotions. "Tactics" are to change when a performer needs a new way to try to achieve his/her "action." A "tactic" change is necessary when a performer literally sees that he/she is not moving toward the attainment of the "action." This stage in Practical Aesthetics is incredibly difficult and takes much practice. The instructor must guide the actors through this period of rehearsal. It is only after this step is mastered that the actors are allowed to play the "as if" to get the "action" by using the actual text of the play. This becomes clearer in application.

Scene analysis applied in performance

In order to fully understand Mamet's system, I will apply Practical Aesthetics to an actual scene. One could apply the system to Mamet's own work, but then its general applicability could be called into question. Given this problem, I've chosen to apply the system to a short scene from a classic American play, *You Can't Take It With You!* by Moss Hart and George S. Kaufman (as printed in Tanner), and the scene is between Grandpa Vanderhof and Mr. Kirby:

MR. KIRBY: I beg your pardon, Mr. Vanderhof. I am a very happy man.
GRANDPA: Are you?
MR. KIRBY: Certainly I am.
GRANDPA: I don't think so. What do you think you get your indigestion from? Happiness? No, sir. You get it because most of your time is spent in doing things you don't want to do.
MR. KIRBY: I don't do anything I don't want to do.
GRANDPA: Yes, you do. You said last night that at the end of a week in Wall Street you're pretty near crazy. Why do you keep on doing it?
MR. KIRBY: Why do I keep on—why, that's my business. A man can't give up his business.
GRANDPA: Why not? You've got all the money you need. You can't take it with you.
MR. KIRBY: That's a very easy thing to say, Mr. Vanderhof. But I have spent my life building up my business.
GRANDPA: And what's it got you? Same kind of mail every morning, same kind of deals, same kind of meetings, same dinners at night, same indigestion. Where does the fun come in? Don't you think there ought to be something

more, Mr. Kirby? You must have wanted more than that when you started out. We haven't got too much time, you know—any of us.
MR. KIRBY: What do you expect me to do? Live the way you do? Do nothing?
GRANDPA: Well, I have a lot of fun. Time enough for everything—read, talk, visit the zoo now and then, practice my darts, even have time to notice when spring comes around. Don't see anybody I don't want to, don't have six hours of things I have to do every day before I get one hour to do what I like in and I haven't taken bicarbonate of soda in thirty-five years. What's the matter with that? (489–490)

The first step in using Practical Aesthetics on this scene is to determine what the characters are literally doing and the second is to determine what each character wants. For clarity, I will temporarily limit my use of personal pronouns. In this scene Grandpa and Mr. Kirby are discussing their lives. That is all they are "literally doing." As for their wants, Grandpa "wants" Mr. Kirby to see that Mr. Kirby is wasting his own life. Mr. Kirby "wants" Grandpa to understand Mr. Kirby is happy living the way Mr. Kirby is living. Mr. Kirby also "wants" Grandpa to know Grandpa's way of life is wrong. In other acting systems these "wants" might be called "objectives," and it would be with these aforementioned "objectives" in mind that the actors begin the scene. I find it difficult to play an objective; it's vague. Mamet wants to go a step further in analysis to provide a concrete "action" for the actor instead of leaving him/her with what could be considered a more abstract "objective" (*True and False* 111).

The next step in Practical Aesthetics is to determine each character's "action." It must be noted that there can be several correct "actions," and Mamet's interpretation of "action" is a bit different from Meisner's. For example, Grandpa could play "to get someone to see the silliness of the situation" or "to get someone to face the facts." Mr. Kirby could play "to show someone who's boss" or "to get someone to see things my way." The instructor is again crucial at this point. Essentially, the instructor must help the actors determine what "actions" are best for them, the scene, and the play. I can only offer possible "actions"; mine may not be the "actions" chosen by the actors performing the scene. Instructors should remember they are constructing a way of acting based on their personal life experiences, interpretations, and thought patterns. The instructor should never make decisions for the actors, but instead question and provide guidance in decision making. This follows the constructivist model of education, where an instructor helps a student build off previous knowledge. Ideally, this makes for a better performance, and functionally constructs knowledge as the system draws from within the actor while enhancing critical thinking skills. Even beginning actors are not "tabula rasa" even though many of us wish that were the case.

After the "actions," actors choose their "as ifs." "As ifs" must be personal, but since this is a theoretical analysis I can only provide hypothetical "as ifs." For example, the person playing Grandpa may develop his "as if" based on the time when he confronted a friend who kept trying on different shirts for a long awaited date. Or, maybe the actor confronted his sister who was hogging the bathroom. Both would support the "action" of "getting someone to see the silliness of the situation." The person playing Mr. Kirby may develop his "as if" from a situation where he and a teacher were arguing over a grade, or from the time he disagreed with a friend's vote for class president. Both would support the "action" of "showing someone who's boss."

The only caution in choosing "as ifs" is to be sure the "as if" fits the situation. For example, the scene may become too intense if the person playing Grandpa used an "as if" that was based on the time he stopped his best friend from committing suicide. In addition, the scene might not be intense enough if the person playing Mr. Kirby used an "as if" that was based on the time he told his brother that he did not need to give back the $1 he borrowed. On the other hand, the actor, or instructor, might want to purposefully suggest raising or lowering the intensity to create a specific effect. The "as if" could be modified to create absurdity, the "as if" could be changed to create comedy, or the "as if" could even be altered to create hysteria. The only restriction is the 'as if' should not recreate the exact situation taking place on stage or recreate a traumatic experience; that is not necessary and can cause an actor to replay emotions from the actual event. Other than that, the possibilities are limitless. The "as if game" can easily be used as a way to test "actions" and "as ifs," too. The actors do not have to feel like they have to get it right the first time. Thinking critically about "actions" and "as ifs" is essential in Practical Aesthetics, and making mistakes in this system can actually be helpful for clarification. Both are part of the learning process, because constructivist pedagogy also supports this type of learning. Getting the answer right the first time is not as important as having an instructor help a student construct an answer based on previous knowledge. What has yet to be discussed is how the actual text of a scene fits into this world of "repetition," "what the characters are literally doing," "wants," "actions," and "as ifs." Insertion of the actual text can best be explained by metaphor.

Although the boat/water analogy has been used by Meisner, as noted in *Sandford Meisner on Acting*, I modify it here to fit my interpretation of Practical Aesthetics for instructors. Therefore, first think of the text as a boat. The boat is solid and is not allowed to be physically altered. Think of the "as if game" as a boat launch. The boat launch is a ramp that provides momentum for the boat to enter a river. Think of the river as the pursuit of an "action" that can change, and think of the oars as "tactics." When launched, the boat slides into the river and no longer needs the launch. The boat uses the river to move forward. The oars are used to shift direction, speed up, slow down, avoid obstacles, and eventually help move the boat ashore. Using this analogy in reference to Practical Aesthetics, the "as if" gets the actor into the pursuit of the "action." The text rides the "action" in order to progress through the scene, and "tactics" control how the text is used to "get to the action" (which is on shore, but down river). Given this analogy, Practical Aesthetics seems relatively simple to learn; however, like learning how to navigate a boat in different rivers, it can take a long time to master.

Practical Aesthetics is not Meisner

At this point, readers familiar with Sanford Meisner's "technique" may be asking "What's the difference between the two systems?" There actually are several differences between Practical Aesthetics and what Meisner taught. First, Meisner's "Word Repetition Game" creates conversation and Practical Aesthetics repetition does not (Meisner and Longwell 23). Let me explain. In my interpretation, Practical Aesthetics uses repetition as a means of observation and impulse training. It trains an actor to "react" impulsively to what he/she sees or is given. Conversation happens when actors are eventually given predetermined text. Repetition trains beginning actors for that time. I do agree with Meisner that repetition forces the actor to focus on the other in the moment and should be done using a "dead pan" voice, but it is very difficult to have a dead pan conversation. In addition, my use of clearly defined levels of repetition also allows actors to gradually develop their skills at this most important exercise and lays the groundwork for reacting impulsively with text. After all, my training at the Atlantic Theatre Acting School showed me that using Practical Aesthetics means every performance should be an improvisation using the given text. Therefore, requiring all levels of repetition to be used by an actor immediately and calling it the "Word Repetition Game" seems confusing for the seasoned actor let alone the Theatre Educator, acting instructor, and/or beginning actor (23).

Second, there also is evidence in *Sanford Meisner on Acting* that Meisner talks about emotions (195). Practical Aesthetics avoids this word. I personally find the word "emotions" especially dangerous to the beginning actor. Focus should never be on one's emotions. The "actions," "as ifs," and "tactics" will lead to an expression of emotions. Early in my career, I made the mistake of discussing emotions I wanted actors to show on stage. In performance, I saw actors portraying emotions; I did not see actors being true to the text. Practical Aesthetics allows emotions to bubble up truthfully. I believe playing an emotion does not truly give life to a scene; it only shows that an actor can fake emotions.

Finally, the most important difference is, Meisner never wrote a book explaining his system of training. He never codified his system. In *Sanford Meisner on Acting*, he notes in the Prologue that he spent four months in Puerto Rico in a house where he attempted to write a book. He does state, "I wrote two chapters. Later, when I reread them, I didn't understand them ... I decided that a creative textbook about acting was a contradiction in terms, and that it was foolish, even wrong, to attempt to write one" (xviii). He then notes:

Friends whom I respected convinced me that my experience in teaching young actors their craft was of value, and that perhaps with a collaborator my ideas could be put into the form of a book. A collaborator was found, a book was written, and I was bitterly disappointed at the results. I came to realize that how I teach is determined by the gradual development of each student. That particular book was never published. (xviii)

Therefore, an outline of Meisner's system written in his own words does not actually exist. We simply have a myriad number of individuals who claim to have been trained by him or by his students, writers who have tried to pin down the Meisner Approach, and the book *Sanford Meisner on Acting* which is a documentary of one of his classes. I have been referring to this book so often because it contains Meisner's own words.

Practical Aesthetics, on the other hand, exists as a system. Theatre Educators and beginning actors need a system to be their anchor. Without an anchor they can drift away into confusion or the world of faking emotions. In addition, without a system as an anchor acting instructors can very easily become scene directors. I often worry more about instructors because teaching acting is so much more difficult than directing a scene. Avoiding this is one of my main reasons for writing this book aimed at future Theatre Educators at any level. So, I have paired the system with voice and movement exercises I learned while training at the Atlantic Theatre Acting School. I also added voice and movement exercises I found to be complementary to Practical Aesthetics, so others may benefit from my experiences. In my teaching of Practical Aesthetics, I finally discovered the necessity of a constructivist approach. Constructivism allows the teacher to build upon the development of each individual student and not the class as a whole. Practical Aesthetics paired with a constructivist approach makes teaching the system to INDIVIDUAL students in a class of many possible. That is why the next chapter in this book focuses on constructivist pedagogy: what it is and how to implement its philosophy.

References

"aesthetics, n.". OED Online. Oxford University Press. December 2013. Web. February 25, 2014. www.oed.com/view/Entry/293508?redirectedFrom =aesthetics.

Atlantic Theatre Company. "About Atlantic; Acting School." Atlantictheater.org. August 8, 2008. Web. October 12, 2013. www.atlantictheater.org/page. aspx?id=12016738.

Bartow, Arthur, editor. *Handbook of Acting Techniques*. London: Nick Hern Books, 2008. Print.

Bartow, Arthur. *Training of the American Actor*. New York: Theatre Communications Group, 2006. Print.

Brestoff, Richard. *The Great Acting Teachers and Their Methods*, Vols. 1 and 2. Hanover, NH: Smith and Kraus, 2005. Print.

Bruder, Melissa, et al. *A Practical Handbook for the Actor*. New York: Vintage Books, 1986. Print.

Epictetus. *The Enchiridion*. Trans. Elizabeth Carter. Classics.mit.edu. 1994–2000. Web. August 8, 2008. http://classics.mit.edu/Epictetus/epicench.html.

James, William. *Principles of Psychology*. New York: H. Holt, 1918. Print.

Lahr, John. "Profiles: Fortress Mamet." *The New Yorker Magazine*, November 17, 1997. Print.

Marcus, Paul and Gabriela Marcus. *Theatre as Life: Practical Wisdom Drawn from Great Acting Teachers, Actors & Actresses*. Milwaukee, WI: Marquette University Press, 2011. Print.

Mamet, David. *True and False*. New York: Pantheon, 1997. Print.

Meisner, Sanford and Dennis Longwell. *Sanford Meisner on Acting*. New York: Vintage Books, 1990. Print.

Silverberg, Larry. *Meisner for Teens: A Life of True Acting*. Hanover, N.H: Smith and Kraus, 2010. Print.

Tanner, Fran A. *Basic Drama Projects*. 8th ed. Logan, Iowa: Perfection Learning, 2009. Print.

Westbrook, Mark. "Practical Aesthetics - An Overview." EzineArticles.com. August 8, 2008. Web. March 12, 2013. http://ezinearticles.com/?Practical-Aesthetics-An-Overview&id=1395198.

2
CONSTRUCTIVISM

Teaching Practical Aesthetics via constructivist pedagogy helps actors and instructors realize that actor training is a process of personal learning and habituation. Practical Aesthetics is not a quick fix for bad acting, because the instructor becomes a facilitator. Therefore, it is important to look at constructivism before I merge constructivist pedagogy with Practical Aesthetics to impart a graceful and effective way for instructors to help students become better actors.

With what seems to have been a boom in interest in the early 1990s, constructivism has been on the minds and in the scholarship of educators and social scientists well into the new millennium. This flurry of interest has also caused a great deal of confusion for me as I tried to pin down a precise theoretical model of constructivism to use in this book. I wanted to make sure my readers were not confused by sources they may have already encountered. When wading through the confusion, I have chosen seven out of many, many texts as scholarly references for my investigation. These specific texts helped me outline a spectrum of ideas about constructivism from origin, concise identification, to pedagogical implementation. I truly believe it necessary to introduce these texts in case an instructor might wish to read more about this educational theory that pairs so well with Practical Aesthetics.

The first and second monographs, which both lie on one end of the intellectual spectrum, examine the origins of constructivism as well as its psychological and epistemological ramifications. The first of these, *Parallel Paths to Constructivism: Jean Piaget and Lev Vygotsky* by Susan Pass, is about origins. The second, *Constructivism in Education: Opinion and Second Opinions on Controversial Issues*, edited by D. C. Phillips, is a critically skeptical monograph about the theory of constructivism itself. A third text fits in the middle of the spectrum: *Constructivism: Theory, Perspectives, and Practice*, edited by Catherine Twomey

Fosnot. It examines constructivism in theory and practice within the field of education. This text has valuable content, but it also was first published in 1995 by the Teachers College of Columbia University and later revised in 2005. This tells me constructivism is still being discussed in academic circles. Then, Bruce Marlowe and Marilyn Page's *Creating and Sustaining the Constructivist Classroom* also fits in the middle, because it clearly defines constructivism so that instructors, scholars, and students can understand it. On the opposite end of this intellectual spectrum lie three books that look specifically at applying constructivism to pedagogy. The first, *Designing for Learning: Six Elements in Constructivist Classrooms* by George W. Gagon, Jr. and Michelle Collay, offers an incredibly clear road map for using constructivism in the classroom. In addition, Gagnon and Collay's *Constructivist Learning Design: Key Questions for Teaching to Standards* (2006) is partly an updated version of *Designing for Learning: Six Elements*. I prefer the earlier text for the purposes of this monograph. The next, *Constructivist Methods for the Secondary Classroom: Engaged Minds* by Ina Clair Gabler and Michael Schroeder, is a methods text for the pre-service teacher. This text is for the secondary classroom. That is why I include it; theatre instructors at the secondary level receive training in educational theory and methods through their education courses. College instructors rarely have any coursework in education, so it is necessary to include some. Secondary teachers are encouraged to use this book when teaching acting because they may be a step ahead in the application of educational theory. I will be using several other sources in this book, but I call these six texts scholarly anchors because they provide primary and critical information necessary for the novice to argue through constructivism from its beginnings as a theory to its implementation. These texts support constructivism as a well-reasoned epistemology that serves instructors well. Of course, before I begin using *constructivism* to show how necessary it is for the acting instructor to apply/practice it "in the moment of teaching" I must define constructivism.

Bruce Marlowe and Marilyn Page in *Creating and Sustaining the Constructivist Classroom* provide teachers and scholars a concise definition of *Constructivism*. *Constructivism* in simplest terms "is a theory that says that learning means constructing and developing one's own knowledge; that we do this by actively questioning, interpreting, problem solving, and creating; and that in-depth understanding is one result of this learning" (Marlowe and Page 25). This relatively basic description harkens back to the work of Piaget who is credited with creating the groundwork for constructivism:

> According to Piaget, the starting point of a child's intellectual growth is his or her own action. As the child actively engages with the people and objects around her, she begins to form mental constructs about what the world is like ... It's the child's own experimentation that leads her to this conclusion ... the creation of a 'schema.' (Pycha, brainconnection.positscience.com)

For Piaget, a schema is

> the basic building block of intelligent behavior—a way of organizing knowledge. Indeed, it is useful to think of schemas as 'units' of knowledge, each relating to one aspect of the world, including objects, actions and abstract (i.e., theoretical) concepts. A schema can be defined as a set of linked mental representations of the world, which we use both to understand and to respond to situations. The assumption is that we store these mental representations and apply them when needed. (McLeod, simplypsychology.org)

A human accesses a schema (singular) or schemata (plural) in order to work toward comprehending all experiences. This "schema theory," the systematic application of schema based on Piaget's work but developed by Richard C. Anderson, suggests that a new experience is compared to existing schemata to see if there is a "match." If no match is found, a human accesses a different schema that helps better understand the experience. The new experience might then modify that existing schema accordingly, or a new schema may have to be created based on the new experience ("The Notion of Schemata and the Educational Enterprise" 415–430). Humans are regularly constructing, destroying, modifying, supplementing, adding, subtracting, forming, and reprocessing schema. We learn by personally constructing or reconstructing for understanding ("The Notion of Schemata and the Educational Enterprise" 415–430).

Reconstructing for understanding

Reconstructing for understanding indicates there is not always an objective truth sitting out there that all of us import into our brains the same way. This is the core tenet of constructivism, and it is how I understand and use the term. Humans construct their personal truths through schema formation and modification, and social interaction plays a vital part in this construction. For example, at the most fundamental level, "Lev Vygotsky and contemporary social psychologist Kenneth Gergen have stressed the role played by language in shaping the individual's construction of knowledge" (Phillips 11). This brings to mind scholars such as Althusser, Lakoff and Johnson, Chomsky, Austin, and a host of others whose theories would be considered part of this societal influence on schema construction. Now if we accept Positivist models that assert there are objective truths we can all know and share, it is easy to reconcile the goals of our current education system. Teaching as a Positivist, we could just continue the practice of having our teachers teach *at* our students, while believing that students digest all knowledge they are given in the same way. Of course, the issue with this plan is we know there are problems with student digestion—if you will excuse the biological metaphor. We do not learn the same way. There is more to the equation than simply understanding students to be visual, aural, kinesthetic, or a combination of these ways of learning. The actual way a learner constructs or creates learning is unique to that individual.

Therefore, I urge educators to consider constructivism to be an epistemology, or a way of knowing, for the sake of improving education—especially for learning how to teach acting using Practical Aesthetics. By understanding constructivism as an epistemology, one can understand it as a learning theory. Then we can teach according to that theory. Although cognitive science is not yet at the point of being able to scan the brain to determine how knowledge is constructed, we do know that individuals learn differently. If we assume schema formation to be individual and based on social interaction, we can tailor education to the individual instead of to the overall population. Teaching Practical Aesthetics with this in mind helps stop the acting instructor from simply being a director. I have had countless experiences in classes where I, as the student, wanted to play a scene a specific way. Instead of guiding or even questioning my reasoning and letting me try, I received the classical "that's not right, so do it this way." I wish I would have had the opportunity to see if I actually was right or wrong. I'll never know, because I was being directed instead of guided. Instructors using this book on Practical Aesthetics along with a basic knowledge of constructivism allow student actors to explore. In my teaching, this exploration has led to amazing product results and also whole classroom learning results. Think about it in this way: instead of directing a scene, the acting instructor not only has the opportunity to let a couple of performers make discoveries using their schemata, he/she has the opportunity to let the entire classroom see how the discoveries are made using their schemata. That is what I call teaching.

The instructor as facilitator

Pedagogy of the Oppressed *and the banking model of education*

The role of the instructor as facilitator is not a new idea. It is our late adoption of this model that is shocking. In addition, I have witnessed instructors in the field actively fight against it. When this happens, "learning" simply becomes a power struggle—and no one ever wins. Teaching and learning Practical Aesthetics cannot be a power struggle, because the instructor cannot live in a student's brain. An instructor can guide schema construction, but cannot force an actor to do something that makes no sense given the actor's schemata. Paolo Freire was the individual who actively wrote on teaching as facilitating; he must be mentioned here. It is his work that really made me see how success with Practical Aesthetics more easily follows from an instructor/facilitator using a constructivist lens and a student actor with an open mind. His book *Pedagogy of the Oppressed* is the foundation that supports the integrated construction of Practical Aesthetics and constructivist pedagogy found in this text.

Paolo Freire was a Brazilian philosopher who taught at the secondary school level. He saw a deep flaw within the education system which led him to name the flaw "The Banking Model of Education." In this model education only permits a single flow of information: teacher to student. Freire notes that

> The teacher presents himself to his students as their necessary opposite; by considering their ignorance absolute, he justifies his own existence. The students, alienated like the slave in the Hegelian dialectic, accept their ignorance as justifying the teacher's existence—but, unlike the slave, they never discover that they educate the teacher. The *raison d'etre* of libertarian education, on the other hand, lies in its drive towards reconciliation. Education must begin with the solution of the teacher-student contradiction, by reconciling the poles of the contradiction so that both are simultaneously teachers and students (*Pedagogy of the Oppressed* 72).

This system, which is still practiced, would never work when using Practical Aesthetics. As I stated earlier, the constructivist model accounts for the experiences of the student actor. He/she is not tabula rasa. Therefore, Practical Aesthetics must be taught by a teacher open to dialogue and what Freire calls libertarian education. An instructor cannot simply teach by depositing information into actors. A solution to the problem can be found if the instructor is dedicated to the constructivist model and uses Constructivist Learning Design, because it IS libertarian education. Otherwise, as Freire would agree:

> This solution is not (nor can it be) found in the banking concept. On the contrary, banking education maintains and even stimulates the contradiction through the following attitudes and practices, which mirror oppressive society as a whole:

a   the teacher teaches and the students are taught;
b   the teacher knows everything and the students know nothing;
c   the teacher thinks and the students are thought about;
d   the teacher talks and the students listen—meekly;
e   the teacher disciplines and the students are disciplined;
f   the teacher chooses and enforces his choice, and the students comply;
g   the teacher acts and the students have the illusion of acting through the action of the teacher;
h   the teacher chooses the program content, and the students (who were not consulted) adapt to it;
i   the teacher confuses the authority of knowledge with his or Her own professional authority, which she and he sets in opposition to the freedom of the students;
j   the teacher is the Subject of the learning process, while the pupils are mere objects (73).

It still surprises me that "The Banking Model" is alive in our universities and schools. Not all teachers practice this, but enough do that several of my students bring their "training" in the "banking model" to the theatre education and acting classroom. Many think in terms of right vs. wrong and want me to fix their acting instead of thinking like an active learner with me as facilitator. When learning to act I learned the ability to guide a student to success, but I do not have the magic answers on a piece of paper in front of me. I offer techniques and work with students. I do not possess A, B, or C answers to the question of how to be a great actor. Therefore, in addition to working with a new system of actor training (Practical Aesthetics) we instructors often must break the habits of the students who have accepted the "banking model." That itself is difficult; however, if we do not try, students take the system with them to other classes and into society. Freire notes how this takes place:

It is not surprising that the banking concept of education regards men as adaptable, manageable beings. The more students work at storing the deposits entrusted to them, the less they develop the critical consciousness which would result from their intervention in the world as transformers of that world. The more completely they accept the passive role imposed on them, the more they tend simply to adapt to the world as it is and to the fragmented view of reality deposited in them (73).

In an acting classroom, students cannot be passive receivers. They need critical consciousness. This allows acting instructors the ability to work with their students in order to achieve what Paulo Freire calls libertarian education. That is why Practical Aesthetics pairs so well with Constructivist Learning Design.

According to Kenneth R. Howe and Jason Berv in their article "Constructing Constructivism, Epistemological and Pedagogical", "In epistemological constructivism, truth and knowledge are established holistically and tentatively, and are not compartmentalized into language/mind, the world, and values. There is no such thing as knowledge *uncontaminated* by any particular system of human purposes, beliefs, values, and activities" (30). This understanding has great ramifications for the education system because it calls for a fundamental rethinking about how we understand, approach, and teach individual students in our classrooms. There are particularly germane points about constructivist learning theory and constructivist pedagogy for the teacher to consider—points I have already integrated into my teaching of acting and promote via this book. I urge any acting instructor using Practical Aesthetics to take the following constructivist concepts to heart before using the system in the classroom:

Constructivist learning theory has two basic premises: (1) learning takes as its starting point the knowledge, attitudes, and interests students bring to the learning situation, and (2) learning results from the interaction between these characteristics and experience in such a way that learners *construct* their own understanding, from the inside, as it were. Constructivist pedagogy … incorporates two premises that parallel those of constructivist learning theory: (1) instruction must take as its starting point the knowledge, attitudes, and interests students bring to the learning situation, and (2) instruction must be designed so as to provide experiences that effectively interact with these characteristics of students so that they may *construct* their own understanding. (30)

By adopting such a theoretical model teachers must treat "learning as an interpretive, recursive, nonlinear building process by active learners interacting with the surround—the physical and social world" (Fosnot, *Theory* 34). I argue that Practical Aesthetics is understandable and most successful when it relies on this process. Practical Aesthetics requires individuals to make connections within the process of acting. They must look inside instead of observing the outside to create a role on stage. In her book *Signs of Change: New Directions in Theatre Education*, Joan Lazarus calls this constructivist methodology "learner centered practice" and considers it a best practice in theatre education (56–62). I absolutely believe this is true. Therefore, I apply constructivist pedagogical methods to the teaching of Practical Aesthetics to provide other teachers with an example of best practices in the teaching of acting at any level.

References

Anderson, Richard C. "The Notion of Schemata and the Educational Enterprise." *Schooling and the Acquisition of Knowledge*. Eds. R. C. Anderson, R. J. Spiro, and W. E. Montague. Hillsdale, NJ: Lawrence Erlbaum Enterprises, 1977. Print.

Fosnot, Catherine T. and Randall Stewart Perry. "Constructivism: A Psychological Theory of Learning." *Constructivism: Theory, Perspectives, and Practice*. Ed. Catherine T. Fosnot. New York: Teachers College Press, 2005. Print.

Freire, Paolo. *Pedagogy of the Oppressed*. Translated by Myra Bergman Ramos. New York: Continuum, 2005. Print.

Gabler, Ina C. and Michaels Schroeder. *Constructivist Methods for the Secondary Classroom: Engaged Minds*. New York: Pearson, 2002.

Gagon, George W. and Michelle Collay. *Designing for Learning: Six Elements in Constructivist Classrooms*. Thousand Oaks, CA: Corwin Press, 2001.

Gagon, George W. and Michelle Collay. *Classrooms Constructivist Learning Design: Key Questions for Teaching to Standards*. Thousand Oaks, CA: Corwin Press, 2006. Print.

Howe, Kenneth R. and Jason Berv. "Constructing Constructivism, Epistemological and Pedagogical." *Constructivism in Education: Opinions and Second Opinions on Controversial Issues*. Ed. D. C. Phillips. Chicago, IL: National Society for the Study of Education, 2000. Print.

Lazarus, Joan. *Signs of Change: New Directions in Theatre Education*. Rev. and amplified edition. Bristol: Intellect, 2012. Print.

Marlowe, Bruce A. and Marilyn L. Page. *Creating and Sustaining the Constructivist Classroom*. Thousand Oaks, CA: Corwin Press, 2005. Print.

McLeod, Saul. "Jean Piaget." Simplypsychology.org. 2012. Web. January 18, 2013. www.simplypsychology.org/piaget.html.

Pass, Susan. *Parallel Paths to Constructivism: Jean Piaget and Lev Vygotsky*. Greenwich, CT: Information Age Publishing, 2004. Print.

Phillips, D. C. *Constructivism in Education: Opinions and Second Opinions on Controversial Issues*. Chicago, IL: National Society for the Study of Education, 2000. Print.

Pycha, Anne. "Jean Piaget: Father of Developmental Psychology." January 21, 2000. Web. June 2, 2013. http://brainconnection.positscience.com/jean-piaget-father-of-developmental-psychology/.

3

TEACHING ACTING USING CONSTRUCTIVIST LEARNING DESIGN

At the end of their article, "Constructivism: A Psychological Theory of Learning," Catherine Twomey Fosnot and Randall Steward Perry issue a challenge to educators. They state, "The challenge for educators is to determine what this new paradigm (constructivism) brings to the practice of teaching" (34). In *Designing for Learning: Six Elements in Constructivist Classrooms*, George W. Gagnon, Jr. and Michelle Collay answer this challenge: "Gagnon and Collay's CLD [Constructivist Learning Design] aims to present teachers with a constructivist perspective on how to arrange classroom events for student learning ... [They] point out that it is better to be a guide on the side than a sage on the stage" (Schmuck x). Therefore, the first part of this chapter examines the base "constructivist link" to Practical Aesthetics; the second part of this chapter looks at why teaching Practical Aesthetics according to Constructivist Learning Design is beneficial to student learning; and the third section sets the stage for the Praxis portion of this book which capitalizes on constructivist techniques in the acting classroom.

In his rephrasing of the "Serenity Prayer" Robert Bella, my own acting teacher, says the actor must "be brave enough to accept those things over which you have little or no control. Apply your will to change those things you can control. [and] Develop the common sense required to distinguish one from the other" (*Training of the American Actor* 229). Young actors have difficulty with this. They often worry about things like "do I look silly?" "are people making fun of me?" or "am I doing this correctly?" This is the wrong choice of focus. By focusing on what one can control, a schema forms which helps the actor put these things out of his/her mind and keep focus on what they learned from the application of Practical Aesthetics using the constructivist lessons they experienced.

For example, Practical Aesthetics teaches actors to focus only on the other actor in a scene. By learning to focus on the other actor and continuing to practice this focus when in rehearsal and on stage, the schema "where to focus" leads to habitual behavior on "where to focus." In fact, this link between individual schema formations and habituation is the "constructivist link" to Practical Aesthetics. Although Practical Aesthetics is a regimented system, it teaches an individual actor how to modify and/or create his/her own acting schema/schemata based on very personal understandings of the elements of the system. It allows acting students to eventually build a single giant personal schema or a set of tightly linked schema about how to act that is/are immediately accessible in rehearsal or on stage. Accessing the schema/schemata tells an actor how to act. The more a personal way of acting is practiced, the easier it becomes; it becomes habit. One might argue that a deliberate habitual activity like knowing how to act can occur by accident, but deliberately learning how to act first requires schema formation. Constructivist pedagogy can facilitate this formation.

In fact, one can use George Gagnon and Michelle Collay's Constructivist Learning Design to facilitate the formation of a student's acting schema via Practical Aesthetics. In order for a lesson to be constructivist, however, each of the elements in Constructivist Learning Design (CLD) must be present. "CLD is composed of six basic parts flowing back and forth into one another in the actual operation of classroom learning: situation, groupings, bridge, questions, exhibit, and reflections" (Schmuck xi). I chose CLD as a model of constructivist pedagogy for ease of application in the classroom. Therefore, I will introduce each of these terms individually, define them, and provide examples of how Practical Aesthetics is taught using CLD. CLD is present in all the lessons I provide in the Praxis section of this book, but I will focus on examples from "Lesson M5—'Analyzing Assigned Scenes'" so the reader will know what to expect in the Praxis section of this book.

One key thing to remember is that some of the elements of Constructivist Learning Design may be similar to elements found in other pedagogical methods. Just because similarities exist does not invalidate the benefits of the total methodology. After all, the method must be able to be used in our existing universities, colleges, and even secondary school. Furthermore, a totally and completely constructivist lesson requires an acting teacher to walk into the classroom daily and say, "What will we explore about acting today?" That method of instruction is obviously not possible in our present education system, nor is it prudent. The important point to remember is that an effective constructivist lesson provides *all* six elements of the CLD. If all elements are present, the lesson can reap the benefits of constructivist pedagogy. The main benefit would be that students hopefully develop individual and easily accessible schematic maps of what it is to be an actor. Each student could then access his/her schema effectively in rehearsal and performance and function as a skilled actor. Thus, transfer between what is taught in class and what the student uses on stage would seamlessly take place. It should then follow that the student provides an effective theatrical performance. For any of this to take place, however, I repeat that a lesson must contain each of the six major parts of Gagnon and Collay's Constructivist Learning Design, a clear understanding of each part by instructor and students, and the presence of minor elements of which it is constructed. If the six major parts, an understanding of their descriptions, and each major parts' minor elements are present, the lesson can be called constructivist and potentially achieve the goals I have already mentioned.

The initial major part of Constructivist Learning Design is *situation*. I include its description as follows: first, the lesson must contain a clearly articulated and easily identifiable classroom endeavor that serves "a specific purpose." Both the teacher and students must be able to easily identify the endeavor with a specific purpose (Gagnon and Collay, *Designing* 18). The teacher must share what is expected as part of the lesson, and the students must be able to understand what is expected and even repeat it back to the teacher if necessary. For example, in "Lesson M5—'Analyzing Assigned Scenes,'" the students are learning how to analyze a scene they will soon perform. That is an endeavor with a specific purpose. Minor elements such as having an actual scene to work with and an understanding that people will view the scene are also essential.

Second, the *situation* must provide "an open-ended task to accomplish" (19). A task is open-ended when it requires more than a simple right or wrong answer. In "Lesson M5—'Analyzing Assigned Scenes'" the students must complete an analysis sheet that identifies what their character is ultimately attempting to achieve on stage. The person playing the character must make this decision. He/she can use a sheet of examples I provide in the Appendix of this text as a guide and can discuss options with a partner, but the decision is ultimately his/hers. There is no right or wrong unless the answer changes what the playwright intends in the scene. Minor elements such as making sure students are allowed to be creative and even take risks in interpretation help an instructor know the task is open-ended.

Third, the *situation* must require focus which "compels interest by challenging students" (20). This is achieved by making sure each student truly contemplates what is to be achieved. The students cannot simply shout out an answer or write anything down. In "Lesson M5—'Analyzing Assigned Scenes,'" the students will be playing a character in the scene. This makes the stakes of the exercise high enough for the students to accomplish, because they will be in front of others showing the product of their work. Minor elements such as choosing a scene that is both appropriate and well-liked by the scene partners helps compel interest. The interest will not be compelling if the actors hate the scene they have chosen or were given.

Fourth, the *situation* "is developmentally appropriate for most students" (21). This means students in the classroom must be able to achieve an answer. If the task is impossible, it is inappropriate. If it is too simple, the students are not engaged in deep thought. In "Lesson M5—'Analyzing Assigned Scenes'" students are making complex decisions about what to put forth in front of an audience. They should be able to provide an answer after thinking about what is happening in the scene. Much like the third characteristic's minor elements, choosing a scene that is both appropriate to their level of learning and well-liked makes the situation developmentally appropriate.

Fifth, the *situation* "connects student learning to real-world experience" (21). The lesson connects what is happening in the classroom to what the students are familiar with in their lives. In "Lesson M5—'Analyzing Assigned Scenes,'" a student actor decides what his/her character is trying to achieve on stage by considering what that "action" is like to him/her personally. This personal association requires students to connect abstract thought to what they have experienced in the past or to what they fantasize about doing. The final step in the Practical Aesthetics analysis process literally asks, "What the character's 'action' is 'as if' to me?" Therefore, a minor element is the idea about the experience—essentially having an idea about what it was like.

Another major part of Constructivist Learning Design is *groupings*. Simply speaking, the instructor must purposely choose groups to fit an activity. This can mean students may work together as a whole class, in pairs, in groups of four, etc. Yet, the groupings must be deliberate to achieve a specific goal. "The basic principle for grouping is that students work together to construct shared meaning" (38). In an acting class, if a teacher only works with the whole class at all times, he/she has not made a truly thoughtful grouping decision where students can work together to make discoveries. Therefore, in "Lesson M5—'Analyzing Assigned Scenes,'" students are deliberately placed in pairs. They will eventually perform their scene as a pair, but there is a step that comes before this.

A minor element to successful *groupings* in an acting class doing scene work using Practical Aesthetics is to have individual actors memorize his/her lines by himself/herself before they work together. Only after each actor memorizes his/her lines of a scene can they be successfully grouped (i.e. placed in pairs). There is debate over this methodology; but Practical Aesthetics essentially calls for, and I endorse, individual actors memorizing the lines of a scene by himself/herself in seclusion before any scene work is completed. The actor must also memorize the scene with NO performance analysis, NO decisions about how any lines will be said, and certainly NO decision making about the other character. This is "dead-pan" memorization. Is this difficult? Yes, very. But again, this must be done over and over again to become habitual and less difficult. It must become second nature to performers using Practical Aesthetics before working with a partner. If we recognize that knowledge construction is heavily social, as constructivist theory argues, knowledge construction can best occur when the two students performing the scene together are able to discover what their characters are doing *together*. In the performance of a scene, it is logical that knowledge about the interaction of the two characters in an actual theatrical scene is best created/understood when the two actors playing those characters provide meaning together. This also allows actors to play and take risks with different interpretations.

Bridge is yet another major part of Constructivist Learning Design. It should be likened to an actual structural bridge that spans an obstacle from point A to point

B. In Constructivist Learning Design, a bridge connects "prior knowledge with new learning to make both more meaningful" (53). In "Lesson M5—'Analyzing Assigned Scenes,'" a scene from the film *Toy Story* is used to connect the knowledge students already have to the analysis process. My students at Arizona State University suggested *Toy Story* as a comparison because of its familiarity. If *Toy Story* is unfamiliar, the instructor can use any film ALL students are familiar with, or multiple films, to make sure all students have a bridge from old knowledge to new. Understanding of the film and the analysis process can then take place.

Using a *bridge* also "evens the playing field so that those who always have the right answer no longer dominate the public domain" (53). Students have all seen films. Therefore, as a minor element to *bridge* I have found films or scenes from films can fulfill a myriad number of *bridge* purposes in the classroom. They can be used to connect the students to information being constructed in a particular lesson. In addition, all students are then involved in learning the analysis process because using a *bridge* can create "community between students" as it fosters collaboration (52). Often students will help one another remember the details of scenes and also help each other make connections. This process also "creates a shared understanding and vocabulary" that can be referenced by the teacher and/or students in the future (53). The *bridge* also "gathers information about what each student knows" (53). The teacher can then determine what needs to be elaborated upon, or what information is easily understood. In using Practical Aesthetics for scene study and performance, students also have the ability to continually reference this example in the future when analyzing scenes. Since I have used a scene from *Toy Story* as a successful reference during the actual scene analysis process I include that lesson later in the book. In constructivist terms, *Toy Story* provided the actors with immediate and personal *bridge* access to existing schema which they can access, reference, and/or modify as they learn how to act using Practical Aesthetics in both rehearsal and performance.

A fourth major part of a Constructivist Learning Design is *questions*. These questions are actually placed into four more categories: "guiding questions," "anticipated questions," "clarifying questions," and "integrating questions" (Gagnon and Collay, *Designing* 66–67). These types of questions are peppered throughout the various sections of the lessons included in this book. Sometimes the questions appear in the lessons, and other times they do not because it is difficult to work with inquiries that have yet to be requested. That is why I often say in the lessons of this book: "ask if there are any questions," "field any student questions," "ask if the students understand," or raise "guiding," "anticipated," and "clarifying" questions so I can field or generate inquiries. In Constructivist Learning Design, the instructor must be prepared to answer questions and raise questions that belong to the four categories to clarify meaning. When using Practical Aesthetics in conjunction with Constructivist Learning Design, *questions* are an instructor's friend and never an enemy. Hence, I would like to investigate the categories of *questions* individually.

Guiding questions are asked by the instructor to understand what the students currently know and to help them assimilate new knowledge via schema creation/modification. They also can "create opportunities for student thinking" by being "broad enough to have multiple answers or several ways to produce an answer" (66). This leads to discussion which promotes social interaction and knowledge construction. In addition, *guiding* questions can "engage or intrigue the students in the answers" because they are based in a familiar *bridge* that students want to talk about (66). They can also function like pieces of a puzzle that students want to complete. For example, in "Lesson M5—'Analyzing Assigned Scenes'" the first questions I ask when examining the *bridge* scene from *Toy Story* are "What is Woody literally doing?" and "What does Woody want?" These are also the two questions students will always ask when analyzing their scenes using Practical Aesthetics; however, the character name in the questions will always change. The question about a familiar film piques student interest and hopefully coaxes them into wanting to come up with an answer. It is always fascinating when students in my class discover that they share a memory. They like to discuss it. The instructor can use that activity to guide the students into the same type of process using a scene they will perform. Once student interest is piqued, it is hoped that they will always be interested in answering *guiding* questions such as those present in the various steps of Practical Aesthetics or those additional *guiding* questions posed by the instructor.

Anticipated questions are a bit different from *guiding* questions. "Anticipated questions can help [the instructor] imagine how students will try to accomplish the task" and should be used to help identify "student misconceptions" before they take place (67). These types of questions attempt to foresee what students find confusing in a specific lesson and answer them before they are raised. In "Lesson M5—'Analyzing Assigned Scenes,'" this question is often raised about a particular scene from *Toy Story*: "I do not understand why Woody wants Buzz to realize he is a toy and not a spaceman?" I know from past experience; however, that an instructor teaching a lesson for the first time may not be able to anticipate this. That is fine at this point. Nevertheless, the instructor should try to place himself/herself in the student's shoes and think of what questions students may pose. For example, think about the questions that might arise when using Practical Aesthetics instead of other actor training systems.

Clarifying questions are paired with *anticipated* questions because they are based on what the students and/or instructor have asked. When a student asks a question, the teacher must pose *clarifying* questions which should "not imply the answers," but "show an understanding of student thinking and probe it, [and] gently challenge misconceptions and extend thinking" (67). If in "Lesson M5—'Analyzing Assigned Scenes'" a student raises what I have come to know as the *anticipated* question "I do not understand why Woody wants Buzz to realize he is a toy and not a spaceman." The instructor must use questions to discover the problem in understanding and settle the student's confusion. For example, a *clarifying* question in this instance might be, "Who is Andy's favorite before Buzz arrives?" The student might answer "Woody." The instructor validates the correct response and could ask another clarifying question such as "If Buzz is actually a spaceman, could that change the way Andy thinks about Buzz?" The student might answer, "Well, since Buzz is a spaceman he has lights and lasers and things which might make Andy like him." The instructor could then ask, "What would happen if Andy really liked those lights and lasers and thought Buzz was a spaceman?" The student might respond, "Oh, I see. If Andy thinks Buzz is a spaceman he might like him better than Woody." The instructor can then answer, "Right. So, what does Woody want to do to prevent this?" The student might then answer, "Woody wants Buzz to realize he is just a toy. That way Woody can remain Andy's favorite." Every time constructivist instructors sense confusion in any lesson they should raise appropriate questions to reinforce student comprehension. This is the kind of teaching that is absent in "banking models" of education where instructors simply lecture with no regard for understanding. The same can be said for instructors who simply direct actors or become acting "gurus" by convincing actors that they must study under them. I often say a lesson is problematic if an instructor is able to "teach" the exact same lesson to an empty room that he/she might teach to a room containing a group of students.

Finally, *integrating* questions can come into play before the students present their work in some way. In this book, it would mean questions before a scene using Practical Aesthetics is presented. "*Integrating* questions should serve as a dipstick or quick check on when to present group thinking" (67). This happens in "Lesson M5—'Analyzing Assigned Scenes'" when I say, "As I said at the beginning of class, I will visit each pair and check-in with your progress." When checking in with each group I could ask how the analysis process is coming along. I could ask if the pair has any questions about their particular scene. I could even help them connect the example from *Toy Story* to their work together. At this point I will not offer specific questions because they vary group to group. The main thing to understand is that *integrating* questions are the instructor's final checks on understanding before a group is asked to present their work.

The bottom line about questions is this: constructivist instructors and those applying Constructivist Learning Design *must use them*. Questions are required for the instructor to enter into a dialogue with his/her students. This dialogue is what makes Constructivist Learning Design and constructivist pedagogy different, appealing, and effective. Dialogue fosters critical thinking, and critical thinking is necessary for more advanced learning and understanding. Learning is halted at a basic knowledge level if dialogue does not take place. For example, "banking model" lessons do not ask questions or provide time for questions. "Banking model lessons" simply present information as so called facts "owned" by the instructor. Students' knowledge, opinions, and questions are not considered because the students are thought of as "inferior" to the instructor. Ignoring what the students know, what they think, and what questions they have reduces teaching to a monologue. A monologue is not an example of effective teaching because there is no way to know what students have learned. A formal test can be a check on knowledge, but open dialogue before a test allows a teacher to make sure there is greater student understanding. This greater understanding might also lead to higher test scores, if the constructivist instructor chooses to use testing as a form of evaluation. In the case of this book, questions pave the way for solid scene work using Practical Aesthetics. Nevertheless, constructivist methods place the student in the center of the learning episode (i.e., lesson) and help them form individual constructs of knowledge (i.e., schema). Students are not fighting to consume the so called "facts" the "banking model" instructor already possesses.

The fifth part of a Constructivist Learning Design is *exhibit*. In an *exhibit*, the student groups present "the artifacts they have generated to document their accomplishment of a task" during a lesson (84). For the acting instructor using Practical Aesthetics during scene work, this means the performance of a scene. This public presentation both clarifies and solidifies what the students have been preparing to perform. After the performance, instructors and other students may also ask questions to understand what the group has done. The *exhibit* allows students to compare each group's work to their own in order to check for appropriate congruency as well as appropriate originality. Not only does this provide a social and pedagogical check on their work, it clarifies their own decisions. Instructors can immediately "determine what learning has taken place." (85). In "Lesson M5—'Analyzing Assigned Scenes,'" students share their scene analyses with the rest of the class. It is important to stress that during this time instructors should determine learning and guide it appropriately if necessary. I did note early on in this book that I was not going to align my Practical Aesthetics lessons with collegiate level, state, or national standards, because they do not exist as they do in secondary schools. Yet, the instructor should have a rubric that gauges the success of the lesson and success of the product. In addition, if students recognize gaps in their learning they can correct those gaps at this time. Teaching professionals can also adapt the exercises in appropriate ways and modify their rubrics in the future if they wish to teach with specific standards in mind. This can guarantee appropriate achievement, and allow instructors to verify learning.

The final and sixth part of a Constructivist Learning Design is *reflections*. A *reflection* is a final review of what has taken place in the classroom during a specific lesson. Instead of making individual comments about scenes, students are now asked to synthesize what they have learned about the topic *overall*. The instructor helps solidify this understanding by reviewing and linking elements of the Constructivist Learning Design. The students are presented with a full picture of the lesson through the instructor's review and connection of the *situation, groups, bridge*, task, and *exhibit*. The reflection must also include asking for any final questions and providing a preview of the next lesson or lessons. For example, in "Lesson M5—'Analyzing Assigned Scenes,'" I hold a quick overall discussion about what we have done and what this lesson has taught us about acting. I also ask for any final questions and mention what we will do in our next class. Therefore, students will hopefully leave the classroom with an understanding of the lesson, knowledge of how it fits in the course, and see how it is connected to their previous knowledge. According to constructivist theory, the students' existing schemata have been modified. In addition, connecting this lesson to the next lesson provides a lesson through line. Students are able to see why we did what we did in this class, where that will lead us, and why any of it matters. In Gagnon and Collay's words, *reflection* allows instructors to "connect the learning episode to big ideas and address common misconceptions" (99). None of this takes place in a "banking model" where teachers teach from bell to bell. A *reflection* gives students the opportunity to synthesize and can avoid students leaving confused or filled with unanswered questions.

I have presented a description of Practical Aesthetics, an overview of constructivism, and a basic analysis of the elements of Constructivist Learning Design. Each will be present in the acting lessons that will soon follow. Left with promising theoretical models such as constructivism, actors and instructors using Practical Aesthetics have a path to success. For me, pairing Practical Aesthetics with Constructivist Learning Design has proven beneficial for analysis and implementation. Application of theory is also helpful in hypothesizing about best practices in other subjects that require teaching and learning. It allows us to be better informed and better trained facilitators even if a theory cannot yet (or ever) be supported empirically. Incoherent systems, no system at all, or classes packed with unrelated lessons that do not take advantage of schematic understanding of the world make success difficult. Practical Aesthetics and Constructivist Learning Design offer a solution. The research I have provided and my own personal-practical knowledge indicate that the teaching of Practical Aesthetics acting via Constructivist Learning Design makes it a viable and extremely beneficial option for training future acting teachers at both the secondary and college levels. One should never underestimate the abilities of beginning actors.

References

Bartow, Artur. *Training of the American Actor*. New York: Theatre Communications Group, 2006. Print.

Fosnot, Catherine T. and Randall Stewart Perry. "Constructivism: A Psychological Theory of Learning." *Constructivism: Theory, Perspectives, and Practice*. Ed. Catherine T. Fosnot. New York: Teachers College Press, 2005. Print.

Gagnon, George W. and Michelle Collay. *Designing for Learning: Six Elements in Constructivist Classrooms*. Thousand Oaks, CA: Corwin Press, 2001. Print.

Schmuck, Richard. "Foreword." *Designing for Learning: Six Elements in Constructivist Classrooms*. By George W.Gagnon, Jr. and Michelle Collay. Thousand Oaks, CA: Corwin Press, 2001. Print.

4

PRAXIS IS THEORY IN ACTION

I have chosen to title this chapter "Praxis is theory in action" for a very specific reason. This section exemplifies what Philip Taylor, Professor of Educational Theatre at New York University, notes in his book *The Drama Classroom: Action, Reflection, Transformation* as the blending of theory and practice:

> For many years now, the word 'practice' has suggested something quite different from theory. Practice connoted the doing, the active, the process. Theory connoted the not-doing, the thinking about, the product. Unfortunately such words, theory and practice, led to unhealthy divisions between those who thought or wrote about drama compared with those who did and practised drama. The thinkers couldn't practise, and the practitioners weren't thinkers, or so the argument went. The word 'praxis,' though, brings these two aspects of theory and practice together, seeing both as a part of a complex dynamic encounter. (5)

I wish to treat the following sections of this book as typifying this "dynamic encounter." It is also only through the use of constructivist theory coupled with Practical Aesthetics that I am able to verbalize what "dynamic encounter" I call learning takes place in my acting and Theatre Education classroom. Therefore, I will rely heavily on the constructivist elements outlined by Gagnon and Collay in *Designing for Learning* to explain why building specific learning sessions using Practical Aesthetics is effective. This melding of theory and practice in these learning sessions, later presented as lesson plans, constitutes the "dynamic encounter" that is Praxis.

It is important to note that each major part of Constructivist Learning Design mentioned by Gagnon and Collay in *Designing for Learning* will be used for every lesson. This does not make preparation unwieldy; it makes the instructor think about teaching as much as content. As I mentioned at the beginning of this book, learning Practical Aesthetics requires habituation. Teaching of the system using constructivism also requires habituation. Unfortunately, most college instructors are not heavily trained in the ways of teaching. K-12 teachers are trained in this way, and we can learn from them. What Gagnon and Collay have done is provide a detailed description of constructivist teaching. They have created a lesson planning system which I believe is applicable to all "teachers." So, I created a template informed by their theory and research that can be used by all instructors who will be teaching acting using Practical Aesthetics or any other subject. This blending of educational theory and Practical Aesthetics offers college instructors and future Theatre Educators methods they may never have learned: Praxis.

It should be noted that in their more recent book *Constructivist Learning Design: Key Questions for Teaching to Standards*, Gagnon and Collay have created a "workbook like approach" to lesson planning in the constructivist style. This text, *Constructivist Learning Design: Key Questions for Teaching to Standards*, does an effective job providing a constructivist lesson blueprint and sufficient examples so a teacher can process constructivism and create lessons that hold true to constructivist pedagogy. As a university professor who once taught at the secondary level, I truly appreciate the depth with which these writers explain constructivism and turn it into a useable pedagogy. I consulted their second book; however, only the spirit of their text is present in my lesson planning template, because it seems to focus too much on K-12 testable standards. For an instructor or future Theatre Educator wishing to focus a bit more on the "how to" of teaching, I believe my constructivist template offers a more direct and simple approach to using Practical Aesthetics in the classroom. For example, other "templates" do exist. The trouble is that other templates I researched can be cumbersome and steeped in educational terminology, and they also may be too simplistic. For example, Gabler and Schroeder's *Constructivist Methods for the Secondary Classroom: Engaged Minds* provides a template that lists "Rationale," "Performance Objective," "Materials," "Student Aim," "Hook," "Development," and "Culmination"" (74). To me, these components seem similar to any standard lesson plan but become bogged down with educational lingo as the authors explain each and give examples. This is problematic for an instructor who wants to give constructivism a try. I wanted a template that keeps the lingo at a minimum, so the instructor stays in the constructivist mindset while teaching Practical Aesthetics. The opposite problem occurs if you conduct an Internet search for "Constructivist Lesson Plan" or "Constructivist Lesson Template." For example, Julie Binnicker's description of constructivist pedagogy in comparison to traditional pedagogy, which one can link to from the Arizona Department of Education, lists in traditional lesson plan format the elements of constructivism:

- Student questions are valued
- Use of manipulative materials

- Students viewed as independent thinkers
- Teachers interact
- Students' point of view sought
- Assessment interwoven with teaching
- Student inquiry encouraged
- Teachers model and coach
- Focus on real-world problems
- Stress on conceptual interrelatedness
- Encourages authentic tasks
- Encourages problem-solving
- Encourages collaborative learning (azed.gov)

These are not incorrect, and I am not saying future theatre instructors and college instructors should avoid these things. Quite the contrary. These elements should be present in any lesson. The problem is that her constructivist definition does not exactly constitute Praxis; it is constructivist in nature. One can see that the list is meant to show teachers what constructivist teachers do, but her list does not model this pedagogy. Her plan offers the instructor constructivist suggestions, but it does not show how to build a constructivist lesson.

In addition, some websites do a fine job summarizing the main elements of constructivist pedagogy, but they lack the link between theory and practice to use constructivism. Praxis is not present. For example, Julie Meek's article for Pearson Education lists the basic tenets of constructivism found in Jacqueline and Martin Brooks' *In Search of Understanding: The Case for Constructivist Classrooms*:

- Students need to be able to transfer learning—applying the learning to new situations—and feel free to change their views when appropriate.
- Learning should center around key concepts, and the instructor should continually assess students' understanding of the essential concepts.
- Students' viewpoints should be sought and valued.
- Teachers may change the instructional practices to fit the cognitive development of the class, instead of rigidly sticking with a preplanned agenda.
- Feedback should be nonjudgmental, and assessment should occur within the context. (phschool.com)

In addition to these basic tenets, Meek goes on to mention the "How To's" of constructivist pedagogy but summarizes in such a way that the reader loses the rich dimensions present in this form of teaching. Regardless, the actual "How To's" from Brooks' text are extremely useful. They just need to be joined with content. Instead, they offer a "user friendly" list of essential characteristics for the constructivist teacher, but Praxis is not present. Now, these are characteristics that can be found in my lesson narratives and templates that follow this chapter, but I link theory to content (e.g., Practical

Aesthetics). Nevertheless, instructors can reference this list when creating their own constructivist lessons; however, I thought I should include the "How To's" directly from the source, the last two chapters of the Brooks text:

1. Constructivist teachers encourage and accept student autonomy and initiative.
2. Constructivist teachers use raw data and primary sources, along with manipulative, interactive and physical materials.
3. When framing tasks, constructivist teachers use cognitive terminology such as "classify," "analyze," "predict," and "create."
4. Constructivist teachers allow student responses to drive lessons, shift instructional strategies, and alter content.
5. Constructivist teachers inquire about students' understanding of those concepts.
6. Constructivist teachers encourage students to engage in dialogue, both with the teacher and with one another.
7. Constructivist teachers encourage student inquiry by asking thoughtful, open-ended questions and encouraging students to ask questions of each other.
8. Constructivist teachers seek elaboration of students' initial responses.
9. Constructivist teachers engage students in experiences that might engender contradictions to their initial hypotheses and then encourage discussion.
10. Constructivist teachers allow wait time after posing questions.
11. Constructivist teachers provide time for students to construct relationships and create metaphors.
12. Constructivist teachers nurture students' natural curiosity through frequent use of the learning cycle model. (103–118)

These take a step closer to content and are valid, but Praxis is missing. What this does show is college instructors teaching acting or training future Theatre Educators can learn from educational theorists writing for K-12 teachers. Therefore, college acting instructors should try to incorporate into their lessons all the aforementioned listed elements, BUT use my lesson templates when teaching Practical Aesthetics and other concepts to be sure Praxis is present. The acting instructor will need to make this habitual. We are asking our students to do this, so I believe we should also aspire toward excellence in teaching. In fact, I have included Brooks' twelve characteristics as part of a *Constructivist Lesson Analysis Blueprint* I include in the Appendix. The Appendix also includes a blank Constructivist Lesson Planning Template that can be duplicated for classroom use. Once content is added, Praxis becomes evident.

It should be noted that my extensive research did not reveal a constructivist lesson template that includes everything I have mentioned thus far in this chapter. That is why I created my own from these various sources. By creating my own constructivist lesson template/blueprint using these sources, and by providing lesson plans with narratives that utilize Constructivist Learning Design, I am able to provide acting instructors with the tools to teach Practical Aesthetics and achieve Praxis. Think of this book as a practical Praxis manual.

The Praxis based chapters that follow will provide a series of Practical Aesthetics lesson plans using a Constructivist Learning Design. Instructors may use these documents to guide their own lessons in Practical Aesthetics or in their theatre courses in general. For each lesson I provide a narrative of the lesson followed by a complete constructivist lesson analysis blueprint for that lesson. Teachers who wish to use these lessons can use the completed template for reference while teaching, but the teacher should read the narrative accounts in order to fully understand what I am trying to convey before leading the lesson. Only then can one see Praxis coming alive.

I must also say I have chosen not to complicate this book with an argument for traditional educational outcomes based on Bloom's taxonomy. Bloom's taxonomy references levels of learning that correspond to depth. I do use commonly used verbs associated with Bloom's taxonomy such as demonstrate, appraise, discover, and infer to indicate the higher level learning taking place. Likewise, I have chosen to avoid an argument about academic standards, such as those by the National Coalition for Core Arts Standards (originally drafted in 1994 by the American Alliance for Theatre Education in cooperation with the Educational Theatre Association). I wrote this book for instructors and future Theatre Educators interested in trying a different and effective method of actor training: achieving Praxis by melding Practical Aesthetics with constructivist pedagogy. This is not to say instructors cannot modify these lessons to meet their needs. Modification, not rigidity, is important because college instructors, and college instructors training future theatre teachers, are still trained professionals who can make their own decisions. I simply created lessons that are true to Practical Aesthetics while modeling constructivist pedagogy. In fact, it is very difficult to teach Practical Aesthetics using the traditional behaviorist or "banking" model I addressed early in this book because student opinion, choice, feedback, and discussion are necessary to the success of the system. Therefore, these lessons do not have to dominate a specific curriculum. They are designed to be used, as needed, by the teacher who must satisfy site-specific curricular requirements and standards. They are also designed to provide actors and future theatre teachers with a performance system they can trust once they leave the classroom.

As an organizing principle for the use of my various lesson plans focusing on Praxis, I have used what I believe to be the three tools of the actor: mind, voice, and body. These three tools must be skillfully utilized in combination to become a successful actor. Yet, in my time as college instructor and at the secondary level I found very few colleagues who taught voice and movement at the level I would have expected within their introductory acting courses. This makes some sense given that college theatre programs provide specific classes devoted to voice and movement. But, it seems to me that all college acting courses should spend some time on voice and movement. Practical Aesthetics requires it. For example, if college students are taking acting as an elective, taking acting to be a theatre educator, or taking acting as part of a theatre minor they may not be exposed to an adequate amount of voice and movement. That is why I put a useful, but limited, number of voice and movement lessons in this text. In fact, in my second lesson I introduce the analogy that the actor is like a piano; he/she has many moving parts that work together in precise combinations to provide "music." It is with this analogy in mind that I organized the lesson plans that eventually follow.

Although the lessons in the next chapters are organized by topic, they are not meant to always be taught in the presented order. All instructors organize their classrooms in different ways, so I do not wish to dictate what lessons should be taught at what time. On the other hand, I do believe class should be diverse and should also build upon previously learned skills. Therefore, I suggest a series of lessons that hold true to Practical Aesthetics and hone the actor's mind, voice, and body—in that order. These lessons can then be passed on to future theatre teachers. I do give credit within my lessons to artists such as Anne Bogart and Rudolf Laban whose work has been used as part of the Practical Aesthetics system as it is taught at the Atlantic Theatre Acting School. Therefore, in the Appendix of this book I provide a 15-Week Lesson Schedule for an introductory acting class. I follow this schedule when I teach Practical Aesthetics at the college level. I found the structure effective for teaching the beginning actor using its "glove to hand" pedagogy, constructivism. Readers may use this schedule or modify it according to their needs. Theatre educators who wish to use this system at the secondary level should extend the 15 week lesson schedule over the course of a year.

Before moving on to the lessons, I want to reiterate that Praxis is what binds each lesson together. Constructivist pedagogy grounds my approach via Praxis because it allows for student opinion, choice, feedback, and discussion; and Practical Aesthetics provides a schematic or cognitive trail for the student to follow. One of my concerns about acting instruction is it can be presented in a disjointed fashion. We do mirror exercises, and then we do tongue twisters. We follow these up with trust exercises and ensemble building exercises. We may then do theatre games, Uta Hagen-based improvisation, Keith Johnstone's Theatre Sports, and finally stage scenes or a full-length play. What we do not always do effectively, I contend, is link these exercises together so students get a complete picture of what it is to act.

Before using Practical Aesthetics, I verbally explained to my students what they are supposed to take from one exercise and the next. Yet, when they stepped on stage for a performance it was often clear that they did not truly internalize what these activities had to do with one another. I found using Constructivist Learning Design and Practical Aesthetics to be the closest thing to a solution. Practical Aesthetics taught through a constructivist approach provides space for performers to build mental schema of what it means to "act." One way this takes place is through the cognitive trail present in Practical Aesthetics. Lessons are linked and build upon one another with appropriate pedagogical theory to achieve Praxis. In fact, I propose that students taught using the following lessons will experience and internalize that cognitive trail from one activity to the next via my use of constructivism and Practical Aesthetics in this book based on action based research. I hope acting students who take part in these exercises can easily construct their own schema and/or schemata about acting and performance in such a way that the lessons come together just like the pieces of a jigsaw puzzle eventually come together to form a clear picture.

With Praxis resonating, I would like to transition to the next chapter and introduce my narrative lesson plans followed by a brief constructivist analysis of each using the template I have created for Practical Aesthetics. I have written these plans in the first person placing the reader in the classroom—an optimal vantage point. The reader can also review this constructivist analysis from the point of view of an instructor so that he/she may replicate these lessons in his/her own classroom. In the words of Richard Sagor, author of *How to Conduct Collaborative Action Research*, "If data collection is the heart of the research process, then data analysis is its soul" (11). This book, then, attempts to provide both the heart and soul of needed scholarship in actor training.

References

Binnicker, Julie. "Education Professions Supplemental Curriculum Lesson Plan." Arizona Department of Education. N.d. Web. October 10, 2013. www. azed.gov/wpcontent/uploads/PDF/LPLP5LessonPlan5TraditionalVSConstructivistLessonPlanning.pdf.

Brooks, Jacqueline G. and Martin G. Brooks. *In Search of Understanding: The Case for Constructivist Classrooms*. Alexandria, VA: Association for Supervision and Curriculum Development, 1993. Print.

Gabler, Ina Claire and Michael Schroeder. *Constructivist Methods for the Secondary Classroom: Enganged Minds*. Boston: Pearson Education, 2003. Print.

Gagnon, George W. and Michelle Collay. *Constructivist Learning Design: Key Questions for Teaching to Standards*. Thousand Oaks, CA: Corwin Press, 2006. Print.

Meek, Julie. "Constructivism: A Model of Learning for Preparing Problem Solvers." Pearson Education. N.d. Web. October 15, 2013. www.phschool.com/ eteach/social_studies/2002_12/ essay.html#Principles.

Sagor, Richard. *How to Conduct Collaborative Action Research*. Alexandria, VA: Association of Supervision and Curriculum Development. 2000. Print.

Taylor, Philip. *The Drama Classroom: Action, Reflection, Transformation*. London: Falmer Press, 2000. Web. October 15, 2013. http://site.ebrary.com/lib/asulib/Doc? id= 10070631 &ppg=10.

5
TRAINING THE MIND TO USE PRACTICAL AESTHETICS

The following lessons are devoted to training the mind of the actor using Practical Aesthetics. In addition to scene analysis and "character" creation, the student will learn how to interact with other actors on stage. Lessons are devoted to teaching the beginning actor how to handle the acting dyad, and these lessons can then be extrapolated by the actor and instructor/future theatre educator to handle performances with varying numbers of actors. To begin I would pair up students and provide scenes for them.

Students/instructors of the Practical Aesthetics system must then work through all the lessons with scenes in hand and eventually memorized without interpretation, in order to understand how the pieces work together, how they build upon each other, and how they eventually function as performance tutorials in their own classrooms. Individuals who willingly and diligently complete the lessons will improve their skills as performers (and teachers) in rehearsal and on stage. The students will also have to integrate the Practical Aesthetics exercises with the voice and movement exercises that come later in this book. To help learners with this integration, I suggest that each student journal about what he/she has learned after each lesson. The journals should be long enough for the student to process the information covered in each lesson. A two-page journal seems extreme, but a paragraph just scratches the surface. I leave it up to the instructor to determine journal length. The instructor can try different lengths until he/she feels comfortable that the student is processing such new information.

Before introducing individual lessons, I want to provide an overview of this chapter. This gives readers an opportunity to view the big picture before diving into each specific lesson. The first lesson, M1: "First day of class introductions," references standard course rituals, establishes course rapport, and engages students in an activity that can help them learn each other's names in a single class period. The second lesson, M2: "Mind, voice, body, and Level I Repetition," familiarizes students with three tools of the actor—mind, voice, and body—and involves students in Practical Aesthetics' basic focus activity, "Repetition." The third lesson, "M3: Level I, II, and II Repetition," reintroduces "Repetition" in its three phases as observational and active/reactive exercises. The fourth lesson, M4: "Practical Aesthetics scene analysis," acquaints students with its unique scene analysis procedure. The fifth lesson, M5: "Analyzing assigned scenes," leads students through the analysis of the scenes they will perform in class. The sixth lesson, M6: "Playing the '*As if* game'" introduces students to an exercise called the "*As if* game." This exercise is meant to connect actors personally to the desires of the characters they are playing in their scenes, and it connects rehearsal to performance. The seventh and eighth lessons, M7: "Using *tools*" and M8: "Shifting *tools*," shows students how to use and change *tools* to get what they want when pursuing a specific desire within a scene. Finally, the ninth lesson, M9: "Rehearsal into performance," is meant to teach actors how to transition smoothly from the rehearsal hall to the stage.

Constructivist instructors reading this portion of the book will split their focus between thinking like individual students and thinking like a teacher. My stylistic approach that follows provides readers with a taste of that dichotomy. Each lesson starts with a narrative approximating how I lead each lesson. Instructors can modify the narrative to suit their needs and the needs of their students, but I felt it essential to include a narrative that shows how a typical lesson might flow. Do not feel like you need to read these narratives aloud during class. On the other hand, I think the lesson narratives allow content to come alive. The lesson analyses, in template form, that follow each lesson retain a formal analytical tone because they reflect the Constructivist Learning Design followed in the narrative. Therefore, the instructor receives both a lesson taking place and an outline for each lesson. It is hoped that the instructor digests both and either uses the template during class or develops his/her own lesson based on the narrative and template. Lastly, it is important to know that class time varies per educational institution. So, the instructor may have to break up a particular lesson to fit time restraints. As long as this is done in a logical fashion, the following lessons/learning episodes cannot be damaged.

Lesson M1: "First day of class introductions"

Lesson narrative

This lesson narrative begins after the instructor has introduced himself/herself, taken attendance, described what the class is about, introduced Practical Aesthetics as an actor training system, and explained the syllabus. I will not provide a narrative of these standard class procedures. The narrative follows.

"In the class time that remains, I would like to welcome everyone again to Acting I in a special way. In the interest of establishing a productive, respectful, and enjoyable classroom environment, I would like to pose a challenge to show how much I value each of you as learners and as artists. I am confident I can learn everyone's name for the rest of the semester in the class time we have left. I can also teach you to do the same.

Please have a seat on the floor in a circle. After you are seated, take a few moments and think of a positive adjective that describes you. The only requirement is the positive adjective must start with the same letter as your first name. For example, I might choose 'terrific' Troy. Please do that now.

The person on my left go first. I have decided to use 'terrific' as my positive adjective so would you please repeat my positive adjective and my name, 'terrific Troy,' followed by your positive adjective and your name. Go ahead and do that now. Now, moving clockwise around the circle, I ask the following person to repeat my positive adjective and name, followed by the positive adjective and name of the person who spoke next, and finally your positive adjective and name. Go ahead and do that now. The goal of this exercise is not to move as fast as we can around the circle, so do now worry about that. Just be sure to say the correct positive adjectives and names. Let's continue around the circle until we get back to me. I will attempt to call everyone by name without using the positive adjective. Let's go ahead and try. I eventually complete the exercise by identifying each person by name.

Now that we have completed this exercise and learned each other's names, it is time to tell you the secret behind this exercise. The exercise capitalizes on a mnemonic device. Our minds are able to attach a descriptive adjective to a person and the descriptive adjective, in turn, triggers our memory of the person's name. I like to do this as an opening activity because I want everyone to feel welcome, safe, and comfortable in this environment.

Before class ends here is a word of advice about our classroom environment. It is truly important to me that we respect one another always. This means we will never ridicule, bully, or laugh at one another unless that is the content of a scene. In addition, I am going to ask you to risk doing some things you may have never done before. Acting exercises can make all of us look odd or strange at times, so it is important that you feel comfortable doing those things in front of others. I also ask that you share your thoughts, opinions, choices, and questions respectfully throughout the semester. If we follow these guidelines we should learn a great deal. I look forward to working with you this semester. You should be memorizing your scenes without interpretation starting now and throughout the class. I'll see you next class." [For a constructivist analysis of this lesson, instructors should see Table 5.1.]

TABLE 5.1 "First Day of Class: Introductions"

Title:	Lesson M1 – "First Day of Class: Introductions" Constructivist Analysis
Subject:	Acting
Level:	I
Objectives:	The students will become familiar with course content (including rules and academic requirements) by going over the course syllabus. The students will also meet one another, learn each other's names, and agree to a sense of positive class community.
Situation:	After the basic activities that start a class, the students must reach a basic level of comfort and familiarity with each other. The instructor should explain how important comfort and familiarity must be in an acting class. After going over the syllabus, ask each student to think of a "positive adjective" that describes himself/herself; however, the first letter of the "positive adjective" must be the same as his/her first name. The students will say their adjective followed by their name. Students will try to memorize the names of every person in class. End by reinforcing the safe and positive environment required in this class.
Groups:	The instructor will ask the students to sit in a circle on the floor or using chairs. This allows each member of the class to see one another. In this case, the entire class functions as a group.
Bridge:	The students will engage in a personal Bridge activity that asks them to bring what they think of themselves (using a positive adjective) into the classroom environment. This activity will be used to engage the student directly in class activity; thus providing a Bridge between individual students and classroom activity.
Exhibit:	The instructor will begin by saying his/her own "positive adjective" followed by his/her name: e.g.; "Terrific Troy." A student volunteer will do the same *after* repeating the instructor's "positive adjective" and name. The next student in the circle will repeat the instructor's "positive adjective" and name, the previous student's "positive adjective" and name, and finally his/her "positive adjective" and name. Each student continues. The instructor completes the activity.
Reflection:	At the end of the lesson, the instructor should ask the students what they thought about the exercise. Was it effective? Enjoyable? Difficult? Why? As many opinions as time allows should be entertained, because this engagement is the hallmark of a constructivist classroom. The instructor then ends with a brief summary and look forward to what will be covered in the next class.

Lesson M2: "Mind, voice, body and Level I Repetition"

Lesson narrative

This lesson uses a piano as a learning tool. The instructor may borrow a piano or arrange to have class in a location that has a piano. If no piano is available, a video of a pianist playing a piano with the top up and slight modifications to the lesson's text are enough to make the simile effective.

"Welcome to our second class of Acting I. You will notice the piano in the center of the room. I am going to give the entire class the opportunity to look at the instrument and see how it works. Please come up at look inside the instrument, notice what happens when you play a black or white key, try to determine what the pedals do, and think about why the top of the piano can be adjusted to various levels. Please feel free to come up right now and do this. I will give you a few minutes to explore the instrument.

I see that some of you are on the floor looking under the instrument. Feel free to do that. In addition, it would be great if each person played at least one key to see the mechanical response. Please do not pound on the keyboard, but do not be afraid to touch it. As you do so, I will pose some hypothetical questions. You do not need to answer them right away. In fact, please refrain from doing so. Just think about my questions as I ask them. We can talk about them as a group in a few minutes.

When you hit a black key, what happens inside the piano? When you hit a white key, what happens inside the piano? When you step on one of the three pedals what happens inside the piano? What do you think a combination of keys might sound like? Why are some combinations pleasant to the ear while others are not? I am going to adjust the lid of the instrument. Can you notice a difference in sound when I move the lid to different positions? Are other instruments constructed in a similar way? What else in our world is constructed in such a mechanical way? It looks as though everyone has had an opportunity to do some investigating, so let's have a seat and talk about the questions I asked. [Hold a discussion which answers these and any other questions the students pose.]

Now I would like to ask you to make a comparison. If I said the human body is like a piano what might you say? [Field student responses.] How is an actor then like a piano? [Field student responses.] I like to think of the actor as a piano because each one of us is like an instrument. In reality, there are several mechanical instruments within us, much like the piano. I am thinking about the mind, the voice, and the body. Each of these instruments serves individual needs on stage, but function in unison as we perform. Does that make sense? Are there any questions? [Field any questions.]

In Acting I we are each going to learn how to control our mind, voice, and body as an actor. That means we must practice. A concert pianist has to practice several hours a day to actually make music, and we have to do the same. The system we are using to do this is called Practical Aesthetics. [I usually provide a brief history of the system at this point.] Practical Aesthetics provides us with a kind of 'ground map' to the training process. I know the term 'training' sounds very military-like, but it is commonly used in the acting field to describe the activities an actor does to become better at his or her craft. For example, Practical Aesthetics offers us a specific process of scene analysis, and it shows us how to approach performance and the acting dyad, or pair, itself. In so doing, we are training the mind. We also do various vocal exercises (e.g., tongue twisters, the humming series, pitch/volume/enunciation work, and others I will introduce) when we are training the voice. Finally, we complete movement work to train the body. I will reintroduce this information and share specific vocabulary as we move through the semester.

At this point in our class, I will walk you through a fundamental acting exercise that is essential to training the mind using the Practical Aesthetics system. I am going to walk up to you and pair you together. After I give you a partner, each of you should grab a chair and move to an open area of the room. You do not want to be right next to another pair of students. Give each other as much room as possible. Let's do that now.

Now that each pair has found their own space, position the chairs so that you are facing one another with about two feet of space between you. You can add a little more space if that makes you more comfortable. I will now talk you though what is called Level I Repetition. In each dyad one of you should be Person A and the other to be Person B. Please decide that now. [Pause] Person A should now look away from Person B. When I say go, Person A should turn, look directly at Person B, and verbally identify the first thing you see. You will then verbalize it to Person B in the following manner: 'You have blue eyes,' 'You are wearing a t-shirt,' 'You are wearing pants,' or perhaps 'You have your hands in your lap.' When I say ready, person A will look away from person B. When I say 'go,' person A will look at Person B and make the verbal identification. So, look away, ready, when you turn try to see what is true in the moment now, go. [Person A completes the activity].

Now, we are going to change things a bit. Person B you are going to respond this time. You will now repeat back to person A what he/she says to you; however, you will phrase it in the following manner: 'I have glasses,' 'I am wearing earrings,' 'I am wearing shorts,' or 'I have my legs crossed' instead of using the pronoun 'you.' Person A will begin, and person B will repeat accordingly. Person A will start and person B will repeat. Person A, ready, what's true in the moment now, person B be ready to repeat, and go. [The instructor must observe and make sure students are actively participating via repetition. The instructor can correct students if they are not.] Congratulations! You have just experienced the beginnings of the repetition exercise.

Now it is time for a few questions. Where was your focus during the exercise? [Field student answers.] For those of you who answered, 'On the other person,' that is the phrase to take away from this beginning exercise. An actor's focus on stage is always 'on the other person.' It is from the other person that we receive body language cues and know how to react to one another. The repetition exercises help you train your mind to stay focused on the other person. Let's try this exercise again, but let's make it a bit more challenging.

This time Person B should look away. When I say 'go' Person B should look at Person A and identify what he/she sees immediately. I would then like Person A to repeat what Person B saw in the same fashion I taught you. Person A, you may keep repeating the first thing you saw, and Person B, you may keep repeating what person A identified. Let's do this several times in a row. Ready, what's true in the moment now, go. [Allow this simple repetition to continue for 8–10 sets of repetitions.] You are all doing very well. You have mastered the basic activities in this early lesson. Let's go ahead and make paying attention a little more difficult.

Now both of you should look away. When I say 'go' you both may look at one another. In that moment, one of you must identify what he/she sees about the other person in that exact moment. It does not matter who starts, but your partner must then repeat what you said. The person who began the repetition will then have the option to repeat the same thing over again, or he/she may identify something new about his/her partner and can say that. If something new is said, the partner at which it is directed must repeat it or identify something new about his/her partner. The goal is either to identify something new you have discovered about your partner in that exact moment or to simply repeat what you heard. One response is not better than the other, they are both equally valid responses. Let's try when I say go. Ready. What's true in the moment now. Go. [If there is confusion, back up and do the exercise again.] Now let's rotate partners and try this again. [Rotate partners and complete the exercise as time allows. It often takes longer than expected.]

Stop. You have successfully made it through Level I of the repetition exercise. If you are confused do not worry about it. You will catch up as we work together. There is no hurry at this point. Nevertheless, what did you find difficult? What did you find easy about this exercise? Are you confused in any way about this exercise? [Hold a brief discussion until the students can verbalize the objective of the lesson: understanding the three tools of the actor and that actors must observe carefully.]

Remember, the important thing is not to be upset if you did not perform the exercise with absolute perfection the very first go. Some of you may still be confused by the exercise as a whole. You should take away two things from today's lesson. First, you should understand that an actor is like a musical instrument, so he/she must practice with his/her instrument like a musician. Second, you should understand that actors must focus on one another when in a scene. In other words, always be aware of what the other actor on stage is doing. If you can take those two thoughts home with you today, you have done very well. Tomorrow we will build upon this repetition exercise to continue to develop actor focus. Focus is the most important thing you can do as an actor right now. Thank you for your hard work and patience. Go ahead and move your chairs back to what we think of as the audience section of the classroom. I look forward to our next class.' [For a constructivist analysis of this lesson, instructors should see Table 5.2]

TABLE 5.2 "Mind, Voice, Body and Level I Repetition"

Title:	Lesson M2 - "Mind, Voice, Body and Level I Repetition" Constructivist Analysis
Subject:	Acting
Level:	I
Objectives:	The students receive their basic introduction to Practical Aesthetics. The students will be able to appraise their "acting instrument" by comparing it to a piano. They will discover the multiple tools of the actor through this analogy. The students will also perform Level I Repetition.
Situation:	The students experience a "hands-on" lesson using a piano which allows them to compare it to themselves as actors. The students also participate in a dyad acting exercise and process their own thoughts and feelings about the exercise in front of others.
Groups:	The students will be in a large group when experimenting with the piano. They will then be placed in dyads by the instructor to conduct their first acting exercise.
Bridge:	The piano itself functions as the bridge which connects the mechanics of a musical instrument to the mechanics of the actor: mind, voice, and body. The students will also brainstorm about other mechanical instruments which come to mind and hopefully link the new information to existing schema. Likewise, they will experience the process of working closely with another actor and focusing on another actor for the same reason.
Exhibit:	The instructor witnesses students in a "hands-on" learning experience. The instructor also views and coaches as necessary the dyad in the "Level I Repetition" acting exercise.
Reflection:	The instructor asks the students what they learned today and processes that with them. The instructor can ask other questions such as, "Has today's lesson changed the way you think about acting? Why or why not?" Various students will have various answers, so the instructor must verbally process each response as time allows. The instructor should note who does and does not respond at the end of a lesson. By doing so, the instructor can ask those students who do not often respond to process their thoughts in future lessons. This is one way to check their levels of comprehension. It is again essential to involve all students in the lesson discussion. Continually saying "guess and be wrong" helps students deal with any negative pressure they might feel by not answering "correctly." The fact is there is no absolutely "correct" answer. A constructivist instructor helps individual students process the information based on their existing schema.

Lesson M3: "Level I, II, and III Repetition"

Lesson narrative

"Welcome back to class. Today we will be reviewing and mastering repetition exercise Level I and learning what I have named Level II and III Repetition. We cannot move on to Level II and III Repetition unless we each feel we have mastered Level I. If I ask if you fully understand Level I, please answer honestly. A 'no' means we need to work a little bit longer at it, and that is perfectly fine. Therefore, today pair up with someone you have not worked with before. This will be our normal procedure until everyone in class has worked together. If you perform professionally, you always work with different actors, so it is important to become used to this. I also want to make sure everyone in our class feels part of our safe class community. Make sure you bring a chair with you as you move to an open space in the classroom and sit down across from one another like you did last class. Go ahead and pair up now.

Today we are going to be working on developing more sensitive and accurate observation skills. Our goal is to be able to react to whatever the other actor is physically doing on stage. It is our job to practice reacting through observation and focus. We are going to continue with the repetition exercise, but instead of identifying physical characteristics we are going to look one level deeper. For example, if yesterday you said to your partner, 'You are smiling,' today you might say, 'You seem happy.' You are interpreting what the smile might mean instead of just identifying the smile. Again, your partner has the option to repeat what was said or to identify something he/she observes about you in that moment. Of course, feel free to include Level I observations, too. You never have to stop making Level I observations. If you are having difficulty looking a level deeper, you can still say, 'You are wearing a Polo shirt,' or 'You just looked away,' or 'Your legs are crossed,' but you should strive to look a level deeper. A level deeper in each of these instances I just mentioned, respectively, might be, 'You are dressed nicely,' 'You seem distracted,' or 'You are relaxed.' Let's try this when I say go. Please place your attention on your partner. What is true in the moment now? Whomever observes something first in each pair will start. Ready, go.

And, stop. Some of you probably have moved on to Level II and others may still be on their way. Remember: do not feel like you are doing something wrong by repeating or remaining at Level I. Each individual moves at his/her own pace. The hope is you will all catch up with one another eventually and be functioning at similar levels. If some of you continue to have troubles after a few class periods, let me know. We can talk over what may be creating an obstacle. I sincerely mean this. It may mean I am not connecting with you. For now, however, let's go ahead and try this exercise again. After stopping, we will rotate partners at least twice. Please begin when I say go. Place your attention on your partner. What is true in the moment now? Ready. Go.

And, stop. We can now go ahead and try Level III Repetition. Level III Repetition asks the actor to make even deeper observations about his/her partner. In Level II Repetition you would observe things such as, 'You are dressed nicely,' 'You seem distracted,' or 'You are relaxed.' In Level III Repetition you might interpret the observations I just mentioned at an even deeper level of interpretation. For example, you might say: 'You look like you might be attending an important meeting,' 'You do not want to do the repetition exercise again,' or 'You think you are going to get an A in this class,' respectfully. The major thing to remember is that you should do your best to make possibly correct observations. If they are incorrect, you partner must still repeat what you said anyway, this is true in all levels of repetition, but remember that you are sharpening your skills at making correct observations. Therefore, if your partner is not 'attending an important meeting,' your partner cannot stop the exercise and argue with you. Your partner must repeat, 'I might be attending an important meeting' even if it is not true. This does not mean you have free rein to make up things about your partner. Absolutely not! You must do your best to make plausible observations. Similarly, you cannot make purposefully mean observations just to hurt your partner's feelings or to make him/her feel that he/she is not doing the exercise correctly. You must respect one another, no matter who your partner might be. Do you understand that? Any questions? [Field any questions.] Please rotate partners before we try this again. [Make sure the students are attempting to go a level deeper than simple obvious observation. If not, provide some guiding questions such as 'What does your partner's face tell you,' 'What do you think your partner feels like right now based on how he/she is seated,' and 'What does your partner's posture tell you?' Actors need to be able to 'read' observations.] Go ahead and do that now.

Now that we have rotated partners let us try Level III Repetition again. Before we do, I have to share a brief anecdote about the repetition exercises. When I trained at the Atlantic Theatre in New York, actors were required to repeat for one hour a day, every day. If we had no one to repeat with, one of my instructors said to repeat with the television. Obviously, he did not expect the television to repeat back, but he did expect us to practice our observation skills. This story highlights the importance of this exercise in Practical Aesthetics. It is a beginning exercise, but it will stay with us through everything we do, even as we mount scenes on stage. If you think about it, acting on stage is similar to doing the repetition exercises. You have a set of lines you must say that are often based on observations you verbalize, but the way you say those lines is based on what nonverbal cues you are receiving from your fellow actor. [Pause for comprehension and possibly repeat this statement more than once. Students are often puzzled by this realization.] We will talk more about this later, but for now let's try this exercise again. Please begin when I say go. Place your attention on your partner. What is true in the moment now? Ready. Go. [Allow the exercise to play out for approximately three minutes. Earlier exercises might run for a minute or two.]

And, stop. [I let this exercise go on for three minutes.] Did that feel like a long or short period of time? [Process the answers with the students.] As you were doing the exercise, I was walking around the room and found a pair of students who are doing a remarkable job at repetition. [If no pair exists, repeat the exercise until one does.] I would like to ask them if we could all watch them work though a round of Level I, II, and III Repetition. Would you let us watch? Thank you. Everyone, please pay attention to [say the students' names]. Look carefully just to make sure we are all doing the exercises correctly. Only one pair will be repeating while everyone else watches. The two of you should be sure to speak loudly so we all can hear everything clearly. Please place your attention on your partner. What's true in the moment now? Ready. Go. [I have often modeled the activity with a strong student, too, to show my comprehension of the system and where students should eventually be in the process.]

And, stop. Give them a short round of applause. Now rotate partners and try the exercise a few more times. Please rotate partners now. When we are back in chairs please place your attention on your partner and get ready to complete the repetition exercise. [Pause] What's true in the moment now? Ready. Go.

I appreciate your work with today's exercises. Place your chairs in what we think of as the audience section of the classroom, and have a seat. Please do that now. At this point we can process what took place in class today. Essentially, what we are doing is reacting to body language and verbal cues, right? What exactly is body language? What are verbal cues? [Lead a discussion on body language, verbal cues, and their impact on human communication. Then transition the discussion to the function of body language and reacting to lines on stage. The repetition exercises show their similarity.] It is often said that eighty percent of human communication is non-verbal. Therefore, in all those conversations we have all day, we are reading and responding not just to words, but to what we are saying with our bodies and with vocal intonation. I did some checking on the eighty percent figure. Some sources say it is fifty percent while other sources say it is ninety percent. The figure is not exactly relevant, but the fact that body language and verbal cues are important is what is relevant. It is all around us every day, and it has a special place on stage. Through the repetition exercises we are able to practice "reading" and reacting to these cues. We will also learn how to control our body and voice as acting tools, but that will come in future lessons. Thank you very much for your work and attention, but before you go I have a question. What did you learn in class today? [Field responses until the students themselves verbalize the objectives of the lessons done so far. Essentially, actors must be comfortable working closely with one another, they must rely on visual cues to deliver lines truthfully, and they must be prepared to react to how and what they hear.] I look forward to working with you again." [For a constructivist analysis of this lesson, instructors should see Table 5.3.]

TABLE 5.3 "Level I, II, and III Repetition"

Title:	Lesson M3 - "Level I, II, and III Repetition" Constructivist Analysis
Subject:	Acting
Level:	I
Objectives:	The students will discover the processes of Level II and III Repetition. The goal is to understand the purpose of the exercises, engage in the exercise, and be able to replicate it in the future. Therefore, the students should be able to complete the exercises and make inferences, during a class discussion, about the role of body language in our society.
Situation:	The students must participate in a dyad acting exercise and process their own thoughts and feelings about the exercise in front of others. One or more pair of students may be asked to model what the class should be learning. Reserve this task for students doing exceptionally well. If the students are confused, the instructor can model the activity with a student of his/her choice.
Groups:	The students will be paired with those they have not worked with before. One partner should rotate to another after an exercise is completed twice.
Bridge:	The students will verbally process the experience of working closely and focusing on another actor. The students are asked about "body language" and its place in the real world and on stage. By the end of the lesson, the students will be able to tell the instructor what they learned because they will be able to draw upon their knowledge of the performance event to extrapolate what the repetition exercise and body language means for the actor. The hope is a new schema about actor training will begin to take shape via the bridge created by a discussion about body language.
Exhibit:	The instructor views and coaches the dyad in Level I, II, and III Repetition. He/she may be required to model the activity, as well.
Reflection:	The instructor asks the students what they learned today and processes responses with them. Since the lesson is structured in an inductive fashion, the students may experience the exercises before understanding them. That is perfectly valid and common.

Lesson M4: "Practical Aesthetics scene analysis"

Lesson narrative

"It is good to see everyone again. [Use Repetition Exercises from Lesson M3 as a class warm-up. I do this for every lesson until I have taught voice and movement. You may substitute theatre games eventually, but allow the class to master Repetition before making that shift.] Please take your chairs back to what we consider the audience section of the room. [Wait for them to return to the designated audience section.] Now that we have had a chance to warm-up, it is time to introduce you to Scene Analysis in the Practical Aesthetics System. What you will learn today should be used in every scene we perform as well as in each scene of every play you perform. It will function as a roadmap for 'living truthfully under imaginary circumstances,' as famous acting coach Sanford Meisner often said (themeisnercenter.com). What does 'living truthfully under imaginary circumstances' actually mean? [Field student responses toward a solid understanding of the acting process.] I believe Practical Aesthetics to be a distilled form of actor training that can be learned by anyone willing to put in the time and the effort. As Melissa Bruder states in *The Practical Handbook for the Actor*, 'Anyone can act if he has the will to do so, and anyone who says he wants to but doesn't have the knack for it suffers from a lack of will, not a lack of talent' (5). Therefore, each one of you can learn how to become an actor if you are willing to work at it. Of course, I will be here to help you. Now let's proceed by learning the Practical Aesthetics Scene Analysis process and then apply what we learn to a scene from a popular film.

I am going to distribute a Scene Analysis worksheet. [The 'Analyzing the Scene: Student Worksheet can be found in the Appendix of this book.] You will notice at the top of the worksheet that I ask you to list identifying information about the play, the scene, your character, and the other character in the scene. At this point, leave that section blank while I explain the basic steps in Scene Analysis and write them on the whiteboard. You should take notes in a notebook or on this sheet. I always have plenty of copies on hand because I expect you to keep these in a folder for the entire semester. That makes them available for reference. If you are using a notebook to take notes, you can refer back to this sheet in your folder as needed.

The first question on the sheet asks, 'What is the character *literally doing*.' [Write this question on the whiteboard.] What do you think this means? [Field several student responses to remain constructivist.] Boiled down, this asks each actor in a scene to put into his/her own words what his/her character is doing without any deep analysis. In other words, this asks you to be very descriptive and not interpretive. For example, a character might be 'having a discussion about finances with his/her spouse,' a mother may be 'talking to her daughter about the daughter's request to use the car that evening,' or an individual might be 'talking to his/her friend about going on a trip.' You will notice that we only note what the character is *literally doing*. We do not try to figure out anything beyond pure description. Therefore, you should avoid any words that suggest a deeper level of analysis; that will come later. Does anyone have any questions about this section of the worksheet? [Field questions at this moment.]

The second question asks, 'What does the character *want*?' [Write this question on the whiteboard.] What do you think this means? [Field several student responses.] The second question *does* ask us to start making interpretations. This is where you, the actor, must determine what your character desires in this specific scene. Remember, we must determine what the character *wants* in this specific scene, not the play itself. If we all were trained in this methodology, we would look at a whole play first and answer these same questions to make sure our scenes fit within the story of the play; however, you are still learning. We can always look at a whole play another day and apply the same analysis. We can; however, modify the answers I provided to the previous question to show how we are interpreting the scene at a deeper level.

In one example I said a character 'might be having a discussion about finances with his/her partner.' If I were to analyze this according to the character's *want*, perhaps the character may '*want* to borrow a substantial amount of money from his/her partner.' If we were to take the example of a mother 'talking to her daughter about the daughter's request to use the car that evening,' perhaps the mother '*wants* her daughter to stay home because she wants to spend some family time with her.' In the third example, instead of saying an individual might be 'talking to his/her friend about going on a trip,' we might conclude that the individual is 'asking his/her best friend to go on spring break with him/her to Mexico.' These examples show what these characters want rather than what they are *literally doing*. Are there any questions about this section of the analysis? [Field any student questions and clarify answers using constructivist pedagogy.]

Now, there have been several occasions while on stage when I knew very well what my character *wanted*. With that in mind I tried to act the scene. What I soon found out is that just knowing the *want* is not enough. I simply find it very difficult to act out a *want*. Other systems call this an 'objective.' That is why I was so happy to discover Practical Aesthetics. It introduced me to another step that would help me discover what I should really be pursuing. This brings us to our third question.

The third question in scene analysis asks us 'what is the character's *action*?' [Write this question on the whiteboard.] This is a little more difficult to understand. You see, an actor should be trying to pursue an action rather than a want or objective. I realize this may be confusing at first, so let me explain more about the essential action of a scene:

> By getting to the essential action of what the character is doing, the actor has stripped away the emotional connotations that might be suggested by the

given circumstances of the play ... The essential action, then is what exists in the scene when you eliminate all ideas about what you think the author is saying the character feels at any given moment in favor of what he is trying to accomplish ... The scene definitely will have an emotional life, but one spontaneously born out of the actor's experience of trying to accomplish something, the degree to which he succeeds or fails, and his reactions to the other person while he is trying to fulfill his action. (Bruder 21–22)

Therefore, the action provides us with something specific we must accomplish. For now, we should discuss examples of an action. If actions are something concretely doable on stage, then I believe it is perfectly acceptable to keep a list of actions that can be used on stage. Therefore, I am passing out a handout with examples of actions on them. [The 'actions handout' is available in the Appendix.] They are not all the possible actions that can be played on stage, but they are a sampling of actions I have either discovered while analyzing scenes, reading, performing, or working with students. These are not copyrighted in anyway, but I learned many of them while studying at the Atlantic Theatre Acting School in New York. In fact, my instructors in New York often said that William H. Macy, a proponent of Practical Aesthetics, has determined that there are only seven basic actions an actor can play. I find that a little limiting, so you will see variations of what many of you might think are the same 'action'; however, shades of meaning can be very important for an actor. For example, one of the actions on the handout is 'to get someone to *face the facts*.' This may seem quite similar to another action on the sheet, 'to smack someone into reality'; however, each of these actions may have a different connotation to the individual actor. By starting with the examples on this handout, you can hone the actions yourselves to be better able to make sense of them on stage. Remember, the actions on this handout can actually be used on stage. When you are given scenes, you can choose appropriate actions directly from this list, but we will undoubtedly modify and add actions to this list as the class progresses. Therefore, you are not bound to this list. It is just a place to start.

I should also note that although you can only play one action at a time in a specific scene with another character, not every scene will have just one action. If you feel like you must change actions within a scene, this can be referred to as a *beat change*. [Write *beat change* on the whiteboard.] You may have beat changes within some of the scenes we examine or work with in class, but you obviously will have several beat changes in a full-length play. Other times you may just play one action in a scene. It just depends on your analysis of the scene. I know you may feel overwhelmed by all this information, but please relax. We will take our time as we work through the system. My goal is to teach you how to perform, not to confuse you, so I will be with you through the entire process. At this point, move on to the next question on the Practical Aesthetics Scene Analysis sheet.

The next question in scene analysis asks you to determine your *as if*. I have phrased this a little differently on the scene analysis handout, but I am going to write, 'What is my *as if*?' on the board. [Write this on the whiteboard.] I will soon tell you why. Please look at the scene analysis sheet. You will see that question number four refers to the *as if*, but I phrased the question like this: 'When did I play that same action in my personal life?' In other words, 'What is the action *as if* to me?' I did this so when you are analyzing a scene you would be able to more easily determine your *as if* by asking yourself, 'When did I play that same action in my actual personal life?' For example, if we take the action 'to get someone to *face the facts*,' you would ask yourself, 'When did I try to get someone to *face the facts* in my personal life?' Perhaps you were trying to convince your best friend that the person he/she was dating was completely wrong for him/her for several reasons. By stating those reasons, you were trying to get that person to face those facts. The only thing I ask when choosing an *as if* is that it must be very specific. You must be able to recall the exact event in which you were playing the *as if*. If that is too embarrassing to talk about, use pronouns only, choose another example, or imagine a fantasy that might fit. So, what are some examples in your personal lives when you tried to get someone to *face the facts* or what might be a fantasy you have about getting someone to *face the facts*? Please be very specific. [Hold a class discussion until satisfied that the students know the difference between the *action* and *as if*.]

The last step in Practical Aesthetics Scene Analysis will be discussed now; that is your *cap*. This time, your *cap* is actually something you must see in your partner. Does this sound familiar to the repetition exercise where you have to react to what you see? It should because you are making an observation. Your *cap* is what you would see your scene partner do if you actually achieved your action. For example, we were talking about trying 'to get someone to *face the facts*.' Well, if you were on stage working toward this action, via an *as if* you have determined, what physical movement would your partner make if you actually achieved your action? This physical movement is considered your *cap*. For example, if we use the aforementioned example of a person trying to get his/her friend 'to *face the facts* and stop dating someone for various reasons,' the *cap* might be 'your friend nodding yes in agreement.' We like to visualize a *cap*, even if we never get it, because it gives us a visual confirmation of actually completing our action. We do not know if our scene partner will 'nod in agreement,' but we know that is what we would like to see. As I said, we may never get that visual confirmation, but it is something we can be working toward. You may have seen the box on the Scene Analysis worksheet that talks about *tools*. We must talk about *tools* after we analyze a scene that should be somewhat familiar to most of us.

Let us examine a pivotal scene in the 1939 movie *The Wizard of Oz*. Has everyone seen the movie? If not, raise your hand. [Be prepared to show the scene if necessary.] Oh yes, please feel free to laugh at my example! I am not using it for its great depth or fascinating plot twists; I am using it because we all share the experience of having seen it. In addition, it provides a relatively simple scene that we can discuss easily. I suggest that you even write down what we come up with on your Scene Analysis worksheet. You can refer to it in the future when looking at more difficult scenes. Remember, I always have copies of the scene analysis sheet on hand for this purpose. Ask if you need one or even a few. Just remember to keep them all. Right now we must get back to the scene in *The Wizard of Oz*.

Do you remember the scene where Dorothy gets to the Emerald City? Then, shortly after that she and her friends finally gain admittance to the Wizard's throne room. In that scene Dorothy asks the Wizard to grant their current desires: she wants to go home, Scarecrow wants a brain, Tin-Man wants a heart, and the Cowardly Lion wants courage. We want to focus on the scene with Dorothy speaking to the Wizard. That gives us two characters to analyze: Dorothy and the Wizard. We will focus on Dorothy first.

If we analyze Dorothy according to Practical Aesthetics elements listed in my questions we first must answer the question: 'What is Dorothy *literally doing*?' What do you think the answer to that is? [Lead a discussion on this question trying to make sure the students do not become analytical.] If we really look at the surface of the scene, Dorothy is simply explaining her current situation to the Wizard. The second question: 'What does Dorothy *want*?' [Lead a discussion on this question.] Yes, at the very heart of the *want* Dorothy *want*s the Wizard to send her home. This leads us to the third question: 'What is Dorothy's *action*?' [Lead a discussion on this question.] If we look on our list of essential *action*s there are several that might work. If you were performing the scene, you would have to choose what your brain and your heart tell you. I find it helpful to reference thinking with the mind and feeling with the heart or feeling in your gut. So what does your mind, heart, or gut tell you? One possibility might be, 'To get someone to see the seriousness of the situation.' Another possibility is 'to get someone to help me'; however, for the essential *action* we can do some interpretation. Therefore, I like one *action* from the list of *action*s better than the rest. I prefer, 'To get what's owed me.' I think we should go with that for now because Dorothy believes the Wizard owes her and her friends the favors she is requesting. After all, he is all powerful; it is not a big deal for him to grant these favors. He owes it to them. They have traveled a long way to see him.

This brings us to the following question. In the following question we would ask ourselves: 'What is it *as if* to me?' The answer would again be individual for each of us. Perhaps you might write, 'It was *as if* I was telling my parents they owed me a college education.' That is similar to Dorothy's request in that we believe our parents owe us things simply because they are our parents. That might not always be true, but I know people think that way. What might be some other similar *as if*s? [Field student responses to create a constructivist bridge to the personal experiences this question has stirred in them.]

Finally, we would ask ourselves the last question. The last question states, 'What might my *cap* look like?' In the case of your parents owing you a college education, they might extend their arms to hug you showing that you are correct in this estimation; they do owe you a college education. I am not saying this is true of everyone in this room; I am just using this as an example of an *as if*. For her *cap* Dorothy may envision the Wizard granting her wishes with the wave of a hand. The person playing Dorothy would provide answers to all the questions on the Scene Analysis sheet.

We now need to switch gears and talk about the Wizard. 'What is the Wizard *literally doing*?' [Discuss this with the class.] Yes, I believe the Wizard is 'hearing the requests of his subject.' Dorothy is a visitor, but I believe the Wizard still thinks of her as his subject. Therefore, 'What does the Wizard *want* in this particular situation?' [Discuss this with the class.] I really believe, 'He *want*s to get rid of Dorothy.' He *want*s her to go away, because he does not *want* to have to worry about a problem he really cannot fix. The next question requires us to ask, 'What is the Wizard's *action*?' If we look at the list, I think 'to show someone who's boss' is a really great choice. The Wizard believes he can tell anyone what to do. We then must ask, 'What is it *as if* to me?' If you prefer, you can ask, 'When did I play that same *action* in my personal life?' Again, this would be individual for all of us, so go ahead and write down a situation when you tried 'to show someone who's boss.' You can simply fill in the blanks on your sheet, if this *action* fits according to the blanks, or write it in the space provided. Perhaps you might write, 'My little brother was having a tantrum, and I would not deal with it. So, I showed him who's boss!' This would work nicely in this particular scene. Again, go ahead and write down your answer. [Wait for them to write something down and ask what they wrote. This is another bridge activity.] Finally we would ask, 'What might your *cap* look like?' Perhaps in this instance, your *cap* might be 'your brother sitting down quietly to show that he has given up.' That would be a reasonable *cap* for this situation. Answering that question would also end our analysis of this scene. Let's now go ahead and review answers. [Lead the class in a discussion about their analyses so they can understand and use the terminology of Practical Aesthetics.]

It is best if we analyze the lesson before we go, and I would like to mention what we will do in our next class. [Hold a quick class summary and provide a look to the future.] Before you leave I have paired students randomly and assigned you two-minute scenes from plays. For our first scene, I like to assign partners. Please just read the scene several times before our next class, but *do not* try to rehearse them. More specifically, *do not try to determine how each line is said*. That will all come organically later. [Pass out the sheets and verbally identify each student as one distributes them.] Remember, do not practice line readings. Please say that back to me. [Wait for them to repeat back the phrase.] I look forward to working with you in our next class." [For a constructivist analysis of this lesson, instructors should see Table 5.4.]

TABLE 5.4 "Practical Aesthetics Scene Analysis"

Title:	Lesson M4 - "Practical Aesthetics Scene Analysis" Constructivist Analysis
Subject:	Acting
Level:	I
Objectives:	The students will comprehend the specific questions asked by the Practical Aesthetics Scene Analysis Sheet. They will analyze a scene according to these questions. They will also justify their choices.
Situation:	The students will use Practical Aesthetics Scene Analysis in class. They will examine it theoretically and also apply it practically to a film.
Groups:	The teacher will lead the class as a whole in this class period.
Bridge:	The students will be asked to choose "*as ifs*" from their individual personal lives. They will also analyze a scene from *The Wizard of Oz*, a film with which they are already familiar. Another film may be substituted based on student response to *The Wizard of Oz*. Accessing student thoughts using a familiar film is also a bridge activity in and of itself.
Exhibit:	The students will show the teacher that they can both understand and apply the scene analysis guidelines accordingly. The teacher will have to provide extra facilitation, since it is the first time they are working with scene analysis.
Reflection:	The instructor reviews what the students learned today and processes that with them. Various students will provide different answers so the instructor must verbally process each response as time allows. The instructor should note who does and does not respond at the end of a lesson. By doing so, the instructor can ask those students who do not often respond to process their thoughts in future lessons. This is one way to check their levels of constructivist comprehension.
Assignment:	The instructor will assign two minute scenes for students to perform or allow students to choose scenes. I have used both options. The reason this is an option is because the scenes do not have to be of any specific quality. This first round of scenes should be used to learn scene analysis, not dramatic form. Nevertheless, I suggest assigning scenes for the first round.

Lesson M5: "Analyzing assigned scenes"

Lesson narrative

"Welcome back to Acting I. [Continue to use Repetition from Lesson M3 as a warm-up.] Please take your chairs back to what we have determined is the audience section of the room. Since you had time to read over your scenes for homework, and we just warmed-up utilizing repetition, we should review the steps of scene analysis. Following that review I want to give you a moment to work with your partners. During that cooperative working period, complete the scene analysis worksheets. Therefore, by the end of class today, you should complete one worksheet per student which corresponds to one worksheet per character in a scene. It is especially helpful that you complete this analysis with your scene partner. I personally believe we should not complete scene analysis sheets in a vacuum. It is very helpful to discuss your choices with your partner. I will also be here to offer assistance. When I give you time together, I will be visiting each pair of students and looking at your work. The only thing I ask is that you do not complete the 'Tool Box' on the worksheet. We will do that together during our next class period. Are there any questions about what will take place in class today? [Field any student questions.] All right, let us review scene analysis.

We will use a scene from the movie *Toy Story* during class today. [It is important not to dismiss children's movies for this activity because they offer us a bridge into the discussion.] So, think back to the scene when Woody and Buzz meet for the first time. In that scene, Buzz believes he is a real spaceman who has crash landed on a foreign planet. Woody meets Buzz on Andy's bed; Andy is their owner. There is a brief greeting between the two toys, which we can get away with playing as a simple greeting. In fact, the simple greeting then launches us into a conflict which encapsulates the scene. The conflict arises from Buzz believing he is a real space man while Woody tries to explain to Buzz that he is a toy. We will analyze this scene immediately following the greeting. As I said, we can play the greeting as a simple greeting since we are just beginning scene analysis. Eventually, you can look at a scene and see if the greeting is a separate beat which requires a separate *action* or if the greeting is covered by the *action* of the proceeding scene.

Take a look at Woody first. What is Woody *literally doing* after the simple first greeting? [Write answers on the whiteboard and field answers from the students. Deliberation and agreement may have to take place for this and the following interrogations.] Yes, after the greeting Woody is talking to Buzz about his status as a spaceman. [Write this on the whiteboard.] What does Woody *want*? [Write this on the whiteboard and field answers from the students.] Yes, Woody *want*s Buzz to realize he is a toy and not a spaceman. [Write this on the whiteboard.] What is Woody's essential *action*? [Write this on the whiteboard and field answers from the students.] As usual, several choices from our list of *action*s might work, and we always have the option to make one up ourselves; however, it seems to me that 'to get someone to wake up and smell the coffee' is a nice fit. [Write this on the whiteboard.] Now we must ask, 'what is this *as if* to me?' [Write this on the whiteboard.] The *as if* will change depending on the person, so the answer would vary according to personal experience. Could I have a suggestion I could write on the whiteboard? [Field responses and write a solid example on the whiteboard.] Finally, 'What might Woody's *cap* look like?' [Field responses and write a solid example on the whiteboard or use the following example.] One example might be 'Buzz putting his hands to his face indicating Woody was right all along.'

Now take a look at Buzz. 'What is Buzz *literally doing*' after the simple first greeting? [Write this on the whiteboard and field answers from the students.] Yes, after the greeting 'Buzz is working with his spacecraft.' [Write this on the whiteboard.] 'What does Buzz *want*?' [Write this on the whiteboard and field answers from the students.] Yes, 'Buzz *want*s Woody to stay out of his way' because he has to get back to outer space where he believes he belongs. [Write this on the whiteboard.] 'What is Buzz's essential *action*?' [Write this on the whiteboard and field answers from the students.] As usual, several choices from our list of *action*s might work, and we always have the option to make one up ourselves; however, it seems to me that 'to get someone to see the seriousness of the situation' is a nice fit. [Write this on the whiteboard.] 'What is this *as if* to me?' [Write this on the whiteboard.] The *as if* will change depending on the person, so the answer would vary according to personal experience. Could I have a suggestion I could write on the whiteboard? [Field responses and write a solid example on the whiteboard.] Finally, what might Buzz's *cap* look like? [Field responses and write a solid example on the whiteboard.] Yes, one example might be 'Woody turning his back to give up the fight.' Nice work.

We have decided upon one interpretation in the scene from *Toy Story*. If you were to perform the scene you might get into rehearsal and figure out the analysis is incorrect. You can feel free to change the analysis at that point. The crucial point is to enter rehearsal with an analysis in mind. If it is wrong, I believe your head, your heart, or your gut will eventually tell you. Are there any questions about the analysis of the scene from *Toy Story*? [Field questions from the students.]

At this point move your chairs and meet with your partner somewhere in the room. Make sure there is enough room between pairs, so conversations do not overlap. Go ahead and do that now. [Wait for them to move.] First, do a dead pan read of the scene I gave you with each other. *Do not try to perform the scene. Do not try to determine how the lines should be said.* Once we have lines memorized we can talk about delivering lines in reaction to what you observe in your partner. Until then, do not predetermine how the lines should be delivered. *It is important to learn there is no exact way the lines should be delivered.* Please remember that. When you are finished, you can discuss ideas with your partner. Go ahead and do a reading of the scene. I will then give you time to work on the scene analysis together. As I said at the beginning of class, I will visit each pair and check-in on your progress. The only section you should leave blank is the *tools* section. [Move around to each group checking on the students' progress.]

Now, since you have done a preliminary analysis, grab your chairs and move back to the area we deemed the audience section of the classroom. Each group will now share their work. Students may ask each other various questions at appropriate points during each presentation, and I will ask questions as well. The questions can help you understand the analyses, they may help the group clarify their answers, or they may motivate some of you to change your answers. Please consider the presentation a check on your understanding. It is not a formal test. There is no penalty for being wrong or modifying your answers as we discuss them. Could I have a pair volunteer to be first? Go ahead and begin by summarizing the scene and sharing the analysis with the class.

Finally, it is beneficial to discuss what we learned today and to mention what we will do in our next class. [Hold a quick overall discussion about what this lesson has taught us about scene analysis in acting. In addition, provide a preview of the future lesson or lessons.] Please pass your scene analysis sheets to the left. I will collect them and comment on each one of them before returning them to you in our next class.

For work outside of class, you should start memorizing your lines. For this scene you do not need to read the play first, but you ordinarily would. Do not memorize line readings; however, or even try to think about how lines should be said. *Memorize them with no vocal or physical expression.* Yes, it is harder than you think, but I really think you can do it. You will have until next week to do this. From talking to you all today, I look forward to seeing these scenes blossom into full production. I will see you next class." [For a constructivist analysis of this lesson, instructors should see Table 5.5.]

TABLE 5.5 "Analyzing Assigned Scenes"

Title:	Lesson M5 - "Analyzing Assigned Scenes" Constructivist Analysis
Subject:	Acting
Level:	I
Objectives:	As an example, I will analyze a scene from *Toy Story*. Students will write their analysis on their scene analysis sheet. The students will apply what they learned in scene analysis to their own chosen scene during this class and/or in the next class. Each pair of students will explain their scene analysis to the instructor.
Situation:	The students review repetition. Students will work as a group to analyze a scene from *Toy Story*. They will then work in pairs to analyze a scene they will perform. The students will then complete one final scene analysis of the class before breaking into pairs and analyzing their own two-person scenes. They would write down their findings.
Groups:	The class begins in a lecture/discussion format, but students break off into pairs. The instructor will check-in with each pair of students as they work on their scene analyses.
Bridge:	The students begin by practicing repetition. They then use their knowledge of scene analysis on a familiar scene from the film *Toy Story*. Finally, the students use their own personal knowledge to create a functional scene analysis for their two-person scenes.
Exhibit:	As a group, the students will apply what was learned about scene analysis to a scene from *Toy Story*. Each pair of students will eventually share their individual scene analyses with the whole class, as well.
Reflection:	The instructor will have the opportunity to review scene analysis with the entire class. He/she will also have the opportunity to check the progress of individual students completing their scene analysis in the dyad. It is a good idea to carry around a notebook, of sorts, where the instructor can write down student problem areas. The instructor can also note students who are struggling. This should not be done to criticize the student, but to note who may require further assistance. The instructor should collect the scene analysis sheets and comment on them accordingly. The instructor may assign a completion grade.
Assignment:	Students should try to memorize scenes without predetermined line readings. They should have at least a quarter of the lines memorized. Another option would be to require the whole piece to be memorized in two class days. I do not suggest this for their first scene because students cannot help but color the lines. Once line readings are internalized, it is very difficult for the beginning actor to color them differently. Keep them to one quarter of the lines for the next class to avoid line readings.

Lesson M6: "Playing the *'As if'* game'"

Lesson narrative

"Welcome back to class. Let's begin with repetition. After the warm-up, you can leave your chairs where they are. I will work with anyone as much as possible if your scene partner is absent, or you may join/observe another pair for the day. If more than one student is absent, the students present can be paired for the day. Go ahead and do that. In addition, here are your scene analysis sheets. I have written comments on each of them. Let me pass them back, and I'll give you a few minutes to look over them. You can discuss my comments with your scene partner *after you read all my comments*; make sure you read all my comments. You have about five minutes to read my comments. Please do that now. I will field questions after the five minutes are up. Are there any questions about my written comments? [Field any questions accordingly.] Remember, I do not want to talk about *tools* quite yet. Just realize there is a part of the analysis that still must be completed. We must learn a very difficult lesson before we can talk about *tools*. So, I need to ask that you please trust me as we move through this next exercise. It is difficult, and it is confusing; but, I know you can do it. I know you are up to the challenge, and I will be with you all the way. At the end of the following exercise we will be able to talk about *tools*. Let's go ahead and try the exercise.

Now that you have received your scene analysis sheets and memorized your scenes, I will teach you the '*as if* game.' The '*as if* game' is an important way to show you how the *as if* functions in Practical Aesthetics. Look at your *action*s and *as if*s, which you should memorize now. [Give the students a minute or two to do this.] To help you memorize and really internalize your *action* and *as if*, take turns telling your partner your *action* and explaining your *as if* to him/her. Remember, the *as if* has to be a very specific event that actually took place, so truly describe that moment to your partner. If you are using a very private *as if* it is fine to leave out the identifying details, but you really are going to have to be clear in your own mind who it was that you were communicating with in the *as if*. You need that for the scene, so try to be as honest as you can. Remember, this is a respectful environment. We do not leave this classroom and gossip about anyone else. Why not? [Wait for responses.] We need to be honest and we need to feel comfortable to share. Do you all agree that this is true, or is it not true? [Wait for a response. I do this because I *want* all people in my classes to treat each other with respect.] Go ahead and take turns sharing your *action*s and *as if*s right now. [Give the students a few minutes to explain the *action* and *as if* to one another.]

Since we have talked about our *actions* and *as if*s, choose which one of you will be Person A and which one of you will be Person B. Go ahead and do that now. [Wait until the students have made their decisions.] Person A, try and recreate a moment from the past. You are going to recreate, here in our classroom, that exact moment of your *as if* as though it was happening again in front of your eyes. How will you do this? Imagine that Person B is the actual person you were communicating with in your *as if*; however, Person B, you do not have to act like the person in your partner's *as if*. You are just a bodily stand-in for that person right now. Do you both understand? [Ask if they understand. If they do not, explain the situation again, preferably in a different way or model it with one actor.] Person A, look at your partner. Can you *see* the person you were communicating with in your *as if*? Remember to do this to the best of your imagination. At this point talk out the *as if*. Yes you are going to talk out the exact situation you experienced with your partner, this time as a stand-in. You will not use the exact words you used in that moment, but you must stick to the *action* you chose. We are just using the *as if* as a sort of boat launch or diving board. Again, Person B, you do not have to do anything; just sit there. Person A, when I say go I *want* you to talk out your *as if* to your partner. I will tell you when to stop. Ready, *go*. [Let Person A talk out the *as if* for a minute or so.] And, *stop*.

Now for discussion. Person A, what was that like? Was it like you were back in the situation you noted in your *as if*? Could someone share his/her thoughts? [If there are no volunteers, ask at least two students to describe what it was like. If students are confused, repeat the exercise and ask the questions again in a different way.] Thank you for doing that. Now, Person B to do the same thing Person A did. Person B, imagine that Person A is the person you were communicating with in your *as if*. Person A, you do not have to act like the person in your partner's *as if*. You are just a bodily stand-in. Person B, go ahead and look at your partner. Try to *see* in your partner the person you were communicating with in your chosen *as if*. Now talk out the *as if*, yes the exact situation you wrote down, to your partner. In essence, you are going to recreate that moment you chose in your *as if* right here in our classroom. Again, Person A, you do not have to do anything; just sit there. When I say go, Person B is to talk out his/her *as if*. I will tell you when to stop. Ready, go. [Let Person B talk out the *as if* for a minute or so.] And, stop. Person B, what was that like? [Field responses from several students.]

Now we are going to turn this into the actual '*as if* game.' That means we have to make the exercise more difficult. I still need you to trust me. This may get confusing, but just follow my directions; you will be fine. There is no harm done if we do it incorrectly; we are in this together. Both of you are going to talk out your *as if*s to one another at the same time. [The instructor should pause if he/she suddenly sees a group of wide-eyed students. The instructor can reassure them again or even demonstrate by being one of the partners.] I believe you can do this. Let's give it a try. Now, I only have two requests. First, *do not react* to anything you hear; just pay attention to what you see and respond given your *action* and as *if*. Second, you *must take turns* speaking. Therefore, each of you can maybe say a sentence or two before it becomes the other person's chance to talk. You know how to do that from the repetition exercises. Are there any questions? [Field questions.] Go ahead and place your attention on your partner. When I say go I want you to talk out your *as if*s 'as if' you are talking with those individuals from your pasts. Remember, right now both of you are working as stand-in and talking out your *as if*s—at the same time. Let's give this a try. Ready, *go*. [Let the students talk out their *as if*s for about 45 seconds to a minute.]

And, *stop*. What was that like? [Field responses from the students.] I know it had to be somewhat strange and confusing to do this. Here we are recreating a moment from your past, but there is someone else standing in for that person. We even complicated that by having two people do the exercise together. You also could only say a sentence or two before you had to pause and let the other person speak. You know, this reminds me of something. It reminds me of what actors do on stage. Actors stand in for other people, do they not? An actor only says a few lines before the other actor has a chance to speak, right? In addition, they both have an intention; or as we say, each plays an *action*. Isn't that interesting? In fact, when you act using Practical Aesthetics you and your acting partner will be acting out your *action*s through your *as if*s every moment you are on stage in your scene. Let me repeat that. Whenever you act using Practical Aesthetics you and your acting partner will be acting out your *action*s through your *as if*s every moment you are on stage in your scene. I know some of you may be confused, so let me take a moment and explain this to everyone.

In Practical Aesthetics you are going to be acting out your *action* using the words of the script. You will be using the '*as if* game' as a sort of boat launch into the river that is your *action*. By thinking about your *as if*, your brain is launched into how to go about trying to achieve your *action*. The difficult part about this on stage is you have to use someone else's words, the words of the script, to get your *action*. Right now, however, you get to use your *as if* to get your *action*. You do not have to worry about the words of the script. That is why this is called the '*as if* game.'

Now, let me ask you a question or two. Did anyone *want* to react to what they saw the other person do? [Field student responses.] Well, you should *want* to react to your partner *as if* he/she was that person in your *as if*. That is the purpose of the exercise. In fact, *both of you should want to react to one another as if the person you mentioned in your as if was sitting right there in front of you*. Just do not try to literally recreate the scene; you cannot because that person is not really here. But if it helps, try to imagine you are having a second chance at the confrontation. We should try this again. This time each of you may feel free to react to your partner *as if* he/she is the person in your *as if*. What I mean by react is you must try to convince that person of the correctness of your *action*. Let me show you what I mean. Would someone volunteer to do the game with me? You do not have to do anything, just sit there and be the stand-in for the person in my *as if*. You will be standing in for my best friend. [If a student does not volunteer, convince someone to do it, and take two chairs to a location where you both can best be seen.]

Thank you for volunteering. You do not have to do anything; just sit there. I will do the talking. Watch how I react to what I see using my words. I am really going to try and convince my partner, who is standing in for my best friend, that 'she needs to see things my way.' That is going to be my *action*. My *as if* is when I had an argument with my best friend about what restaurant we were going to go to last week. Please pay attention as I do this. [I start talking out my *as if* to the student. If the student looks away I might say, 'Stop looking away. I am trying to get you to see things my way.' If the person smiles I might say, 'Why are you smiling? I'm the one who is right in this conversation. You look like you are dressed up to go to that expensive Italian restaurant we always go to. I do not *want* Italian food. It is loaded with calories, and we just should not eat it. Stop smiling! I'm being serious here. I am concerned about our health. Ok, fine, then keep smiling. Now you are making me feel terrible. All I care about is our health. I do not want you to have a heart attack next year. Can you understand that? Why can't you see things my way? We always have Italian. You should let me choose this time.' Then I might say, 'How can you not see things my way?' The students should recognize what is going on as something that looks like the repetition exercises. If not, stop and point this out. Then help the students make the connection.]

Now, what you saw me do looked like something we have been doing for quite a while now. In fact you did it at the beginning of class today. What was that? [The students should say repetition.] Yes, what you saw should have resembled a mix between the repetition exercise and talking out the *as if*. Did it look like that to you? [Field responses. If they were unconvinced, try to convince them of the fact. If they are not convinced, have them repeat my example. This time I would use different words, but still try to get that person 'to see things my way.'] Now it is your turn. [Thank the volunteer and ask her to return to her partner.] Try this exercise again. Person A, do just what I did; mix the repetition exercise with talking out the *as if*. Person B, all you must do is sit there. Let's try this when I say go. Ready, go. [Let Person A talk for a minute or two.]

And, *stop*. Now it is time to give Person B a chance. Person B, do the same thing; mix the repetition exercise with talking out the *as if*. Person A, all you have to do is sit there. Let's try this when I say *go*. Ready, *go*. [Let Person B talk for a minute or two.] And, *stop*. What was that like? [Field student responses accordingly.] What you were doing was starting to work with different tactics to get your *action*. In Practical Aesthetics, we call these tactics *tools*. If you were trying to convince your partner by begging, you were using begging as a tool. If you were reasoning with your partner, you were using reasoning as a tool. If you were joking, you were using joking as a tool. If you were bribing your partner into believing your *action*, you were using bribery as a tool.

I will summarize what we just did and what we will always call the '*as if* game.' Each of you was playing an *action* through an *as if*. When you shifted how you were playing the *action* based on what your partner was doing physically, you changed your tool to attain your *action*. That is the essence of the '*as if* game.' Two people play the '*as if* game' by trying to get their *actions* through and *as if*s by using various *tools*. I actually have a list of *tools* that everyone must have. Give me a second to pass it out. [Pass out the 'Some Examples of *Tools*' handout found in the Appendix.] In other words, *tools* are really your tactics to get your *action*. In the '*as if* game' each player tries to achieve an *action* by talking out an *as if*. When a player changes *tools* to get his/her *action* he/she is using a different approach to get his/her *action*. That is the '*as if* game.' You will see several *tools* on the list I just gave you, but this is not a list of all possible *tools*. This list just gives you a start like the list of *action*s did. You can use these *tools* in your scene, and you can add to the list any *tools* you discover. You see, the '*as if* game's' function is to get us into the text of the scene, but that is for another class. I do not *want* to discuss that right now. I just *want* you to know you just learned the '*as if* game.' Do you think you could do it again next class? Why? Please explain it to me [Field responses appropriately.] We will start with the '*as if* game' next class.

Go ahead and put your chairs back in what we consider the audience section of the room and give me your attention for a moment. [Give the students time to do this.] Today's work may have been confusing and difficult. If you are still confused, please do not worry. Sometimes it takes a few days for everything to make complete sense. Remember, everyone is different; people work at different speeds to learn different skills. What I *want* you to know is that each of you can master the '*as if* game' eventually. Next class we will practice the '*as if* game' and learn how to shift *tools* more easily. There is no new homework for tonight, just make sure you keep your scene memorized and bring your 'Scene Analysis Sheet' and your 'Some Examples of *Tools*' handout to class next time. Just remember two things about Practical Aesthetics. First, an actor works through the *as if* to achieve his/her *action*. Second, when the actor changes an approach to get that *action*, he/she is changing *tools*. [Repeat these two things and ask the students to be ready to repeat them back at the beginning of our next class.] I will see you soon." [For a constructivist analysis of this lesson, instructors should see Table 5.6.]

TABLE 5.6 "Playing the '*As if* Game'"

Title:	Lesson M6 - "Playing the *as if* Game" Constructivist Analysis
Subject:	Acting
Level:	I
Objectives:	Each student in a dyad will explain his/her *action* and "*as if*" to each other. Each student will perform work toward the *action* by talking out the "*as if.*" Each student will recognize our acting exercises as parts of the actual on stage acting experience. The dyad will be able to perform the "*as ifs*" at the same time. The students will be able to summarize the Practical Aesthetics acting system as working toward an *action* through an "*as if*" by using "*tools.*"
Situation:	The students will learn a new exercise: the "*as if* game." The students must perform the "*as if* game" and understand its place in Practical Aesthetics and acting as a whole.
Groups:	The class will be a mixture of lecture/discussion and dyad exercises. The instructor will also model the "*as if* game" by performing it with a student.
Bridge:	The students explain their own "*actions*" and "*as ifs*" to one another. This allows them to process their own experiences or fantasies within the acting exercise. They will then perform their own experience, which will show them that they can draw upon their own experience in acting instead of trying to be someone else.
Exhibit:	Students will explain their "*actions*" and "*as ifs*" to their partners in the dyad. The teacher will evaluate the students' performance of the "*as if* game." The instructor will also model the "*as if* game." The exhibit is of utmost importance to the understanding of Practical Aesthetics, so the instructor must keep focus on each and every student. The instructor cannot let any student remain inactive. Inactivity is the only real danger in this system. If a student does not participate there is no way he/she can learn the system. The teacher must be extremely sensitive to this.
Reflection:	The key to the success of this lesson is continual reflection on what is taking place. In order to check for understanding, ask students to verbalize what they are doing and learning in the lesson.
Assignment:	The students must keep one quarter of their scene memorized, they must bring their Scene Analysis Sheets to the next class, and they must also bring their "Some Examples of *Tools*" handout to the next class.

Lesson M7: "Using *tools*"

Lesson narrative

"Welcome back to class. Again, let's begin with repetition [Repetition is Lesson M3.] Choose a partner and begin. [Stop repetition after a few minutes.]. Today we are going to learn another essential step in the Practical Aesthetics system: using *tools* proficiently. In our last class I handed back your Scene Analysis worksheet, and I distributed a handout labeled 'Some Examples of *Tools*.' I also explained *tools*, but I *want* to focus on them again. If you would, please go get those papers and come back to the chairs which are already in place from repetition exercises. When you return, however, please sit with your scene partner.

If you remember from our last class we discussed a basic definition of *tools*. Would someone please share that definition with me? What do you remember? [Field student responses and make sure they understand the definition of *tools*.] Now, I also ended our class by saying you should remember two things. What were those two things? I am just curious about what you remember. [Field student responses but expect them to be a bit unclear. Then repeat the two things they were asked to remember.] Well, the first concept I asked you to remember was *an actor works through the as if to achieve his/her action*. The second concept I asked you to remember was *when an actor changes an approach to get that action, he/she is changing tools*. Therefore, in the '*as if* game,' we learned how to talk through the *as if* with the intent to achieve our *action* and possibly see our *cap*. If you remember, the *cap* is the physical gesture your partner might physically do that means you achieved your *action*; although, you may never see that *cap*. Well, today we are going to do the same basic exercise but move one step ahead. Today, I am going to teach you how to use the '*as if* game' as a boat launch into the text of your actual scene. That also means we must practice using *tools*. If you have seen a boat launch, it resembles a ramp. An owner places his/her boat at the launch and allows the boat to slide into the water with momentum. Our goal today is to allow the '*as if* game' to launch us into working toward our *action* with momentum provided by the *as if*; however, instead of improvising the words of the *as if* for the whole exercise, we are going to eventually use the text of the scene. Yes, we are once again making an exercise just a little bit more difficult. Just do not lose confidence; I believe you can do it. Always remember, it is perfectly fine to 'guess and be wrong' in this class. That is how we learn. Let's give it a try.

To begin, we are going to play the '*as if* game' we learned in our last class. I think we should practice that once or twice before we move forward. [Run the students through the '*as if* game' at least twice.] I also asked you to memorize text from your scene. Now it is time to do a run-through of that dialogue. Remember, *do not act the lines*. At this point, just do an expressionless reading with your partner.

[Ask them to rehearse the lines twice or three times in monotone voices just to be certain they have at least a quarter of the lines down very quickly.] Now, pay close attention as I explain the following steps.

Begin the '*as if* game' as we have always done. After you are well into the exercise, I will say *line*. At that exact point I *want* you all to shift from improvising in the *as if* to using the opening lines of text from your scene. Therefore, when I say *line* the partner who has the first line of the scene would say his/her first line followed by his/her partner saying his/her first line. You would go through the scene as far as you remember. The key is wherever you are vocally, physically, or even spiritually in the improvisation of the '*as if* game,' you must shift that vocal, physical, or spiritual *color* to the lines of your scene. What you are doing is using the improvised '*as if* game' to launch yourself vocally, physically, and spiritually into the scene. That is why I did not *want* you to come up with line readings. I also do not *want* you to plug in emotions. This is not emotion recall. Emotional responses will always change depending on where you are in the '*as if* game' based on what you receive from your partner. All you need to worry about is continuing to work toward achieving your *action* using your lines, which will now be colored by your *as if* improvisation. Does this make sense? [Field student responses, because this is a difficult concept to grasp. It might take the students a while to understand. Rephrase and repeat before going ahead with the exercise. In addition, ask very *ca*pable students to demonstrate.] Go ahead and try.

First, place your attention on your partner. I will now start posing the following question before we begin any '*as if* game': *What is true in the moment now?* I learned this phrase from Robert Bella and Paul Urcioli, my acting instructors at the Atlantic Theatre in New York. What I am asking is that you mentally identify, like we did verbally in repetition, what you see in your partner at this very moment. Essentially, what is true to you right now? For example, if you are playing the *action* 'to get someone to wake up and smell the coffee,' does your partner look like he/she is ready 'to wake up and smell the coffee?' If so, you can begin talking out your *as if* as though you have achieved your goal; your partner has 'woken up and smelled the coffee.' Your job is only to make sure he/she stays in that state of being. If he/she is in any other state of being (perhaps he/she looks as though he/she is confused) you have some convincing to do. That means you have to decide what you first *want* to say to try and convince him/her 'to wake up and smell the coffee.' You also must decide how you are going to say it; however, you can only decide what to say and how to say it when you mentally identify what you see in your partner at this moment. Does that make sense? [Field any questions and/or try explaining this again in different words if necessary.] All of us will try this exercise. When I say *go*, begin the '*as if* game.' When I say line, you are to shift into the text of your scene. Get ready ... what is true in the moment now? Ready, go! [Let the '*as if* game' go on for a minute or so before saying line.] Line! [Let the scene go until the students do not remember any of their lines. It is customary for them to forget their first line even after several tries. Just keep trying until they make the shift into the scene. It may take some effort for them to do so.] And, stop. Now, let's talk about this. Tell me what that was like. [Field student responses. There is no wrong answer.] I appreciate your honesty. That was a challenging task to complete.

I now have a question for you. When you shifted into using the lines of the scene, how would you describe the tool you were using? In other words, try to think back and recall the tactic you used to try and convince your partner. To help you remember, look at the 'Some Examples of *Tools*' handout I asked that you have with you. Do any of the *tools* listed on the sheet describe how you were coloring your lines? [Field responses from the students. If no one answers, start reading down the list of *tools*. Sometimes recognition happens aurally rather than visually. If there is still no response, run the exercise again before asking about *tools* again. In fact, run the exercise again even if huge moments of realization happen. There is nothing wrong with doing any Practical Aesthetics exercise multiple times.] Some of you did recognize that you were flattering, reasoning, and even threatening your scene partner with some of your lines. [The examples depend upon student feedback.] I appreciate you taking the time to really think about what you were saying and how you said it. What would you say if I told you that now, instead of accidentally falling into the use of a tool, you can actually choose which ones to use? [Repeat the question and field responses.] Yes. Instead of having to stumble upon an approach you can use the *tools* on this list, or those you discover, to 'color' your lines. You just must never play an emotion; emotion will be present to the audience without your help. Let me explain.

Do you remember back in the repetition exercises when you 'read' your partner? I am sure you know what I mean because you were able to say things like 'you are enjoying yourself,' 'you think you are good at this,' and 'you think you are winning this game.' Likewise, remember when we first learned the '*as if* game' and you shifted how you were playing the *action* based on what your partner was doing physically. I said you changed your tool to attain your *action*. Well, what we did today was the first step in integrating all these pieces of the puzzle we have learned since we started. Today, we discovered how *tools* actually function. Therefore, you must choose a tool that appropriately responds to what you see in your partner. Eventually, you will become so good at this that the *as if* will simply function as a mnemonic to get you into trying to achieve your *action* by using specific *tools*. Instead of improvising words of the '*as if*,' you will use the lines of your scene colored by *tools*. Again, the *tools* you choose will be based on what you see in your partner at that moment. For example, if you are trying 'to get what's owed me' and your partner looks like he/she is ready to cry, you might try using the lines of the scene colored by 'flattery' to get your *action*. On the other hand, if you are trying 'to get what's owed me' and your partner is laughing, you might try using the lines of the scene colored by 'bribery' to bribe your partner into giving you 'what's owed you.' Do you follow me? [Field responses. Everyone might totally understand, or no one might understand; every group is different. Regardless, repeat this entire exercise for a reasonable period. Even if no one understands, they have had the experience. It may become clearer to them after they think about it for a while.]

Please move your chairs back to what we have deemed the audience section of the classroom and have a seat. Keep your Scene Analysis Sheet and *Tools* handout nearby because I *want* to talk about them. Since we all have had the experience of using *tools*, take a look at your 'Scene Analysis Sheet.' Do you remember the box I told you to leave blank? It is labeled, 'What are the *tools* you might use to complete your *action* or achieve your *cap?*' Right now, just for the sake of argument, write down three or four *tools* that might help you achieve your *action* in your scene. Do that now. [Give the students a moment to write that down.] Remember, your choice of tool is dependent on how you read your partner 'in the moment' so you may never use those *tools* you wrote down. Nevertheless, you now understand what they are and how they work. Since you wrote them down, you can look at these examples next time to remember what *tools* are and how they work. For your assignment, memorize lines you may have missed.

You now realize how difficult it can be to remember your lines in Practical Aesthetics, so you must practice learning your lines. When we meet again, we will need the whole scene memorized perfectly because we will do the exact same activity we did today, except I will show you exactly how to switch *tools* in a scene. For now, if you are still confused about the work we are doing in class please do not worry about it. Just memorize your lines. The rest will come. Everyone learns at a different pace. The key is you cannot give up on the system. Practical Aesthetics is useful only if you practice perseverance and never give up. I will be here with you the whole time.

So, next class we will play the '*as if* game,' we will shift into the lines of your scene, and we will learn how to shift *tools*. Trust me. I realize all of this is difficult, but I congratulate all of you on your work. Acting is just plain difficult; that is why it feels so great when you finally succeed! The only way you can succeed, however, is to persevere. I will see you next class." [For a constructivist analysis of this lesson, instructors should see Table 5.7.]

TABLE 5.7 "Using *Tools*"

Title:	Lesson M7 - "Using *Tools*" Constructivist Analysis
Subject:	Acting
Level:	I
Objectives:	The students will be able to evaluate the purpose of "*tools*." The students will apply the "*as if* game" as a "launch" into the "*action*." The students will gain an appreciation for the use of "tool shifting" in a scene. The students will combine various class elements to work for them in the beginning stages of rehearsing a scene.
Situation:	The class will begin with a dyad of repetition. There will be some lecture discussion, but ultimately activities will be confined to the dyad consisting of scene partners. The scene partners will be expected to use the "*as if* game" as a way of getting into their scene and using their lines to achieve their "*action*s."
Groups:	The students will work in two different dyads. One for the repetition exercise and a second with their scene partners. The last portion of class will be spent with the instructor addressing the class as a whole.
Bridge:	Major bridge activities take place in this lesson. Students will once again use repetition to understand the new activities they will be completing. In addition, a cognitive link will be reinforced between what was covered in past lessons about "*action*s" and "*as if*s" and what the students will learn about "*tools*" today. Lastly, individual student "*as if*s" will be used to jump into dialogue. This links personal experience to the use of lines from a script. This is a base reason why I consider Practical Aesthetics to be constructivist in nature.
Exhibit:	The instructor will see the very beginnings of a dyad's scene performance. He/she will be able to evaluate their use of "*action*s," "*as if*s," and "*tools*" as they begin to apply them to a dramatic text. The instructor will also be able to evaluate how well the students shift from the "*as if*" to the lines of the actual scene they will be performing.
Reflection:	At various points the instructor will check for student understanding. If the students fully understand, great. If the students have trouble, that is fine, too. The instructor must persevere with the students. He/she must push them to literally try and fail. It is through this personal student processing and trial and error that the students will become adept at Practical Aesthetics. The instructor must realize that the students may need a day or two for the brain to process/memorize various activities. The mind is complex; we must be open to its processes. A constructivist teacher is open to the active construction of knowledge.
Assignment:	The students should memorize the rest of their scenes.

lesson M8: "Shifting *Tools*"

Lesson narrative

"Hello everyone; welcome back. Get chairs and sit with your scene partner, because you guessed it; it is time for repetition. [Repetition is found in Lesson M3.] We will do repetition exercises for approximately five minutes and then continue. [Walk around and make sure the students are doing the repetition exercises. At this point, they may be a little tired of the exercise. They just do not know how important it is.] In our last lesson we learned how to use *tools*. If you remember, I said that the '*as if* game' is like a boat launch that launches us into pursuing the *action* we have chosen in our scene. If that is the case, then *tools* become the oars of the boat. You would use *tools* to propel yourself through the actual activity of trying to achieve your *action*. Like oars, *tools* can help you change direction, move in a circle, speed up, slow down, or even stop. Therefore, today we *want* to learn how to use and shift *tools* to do these things I just mentioned. It may seem like we are spending an extended amount of time on *tools*. I have found that to be necessary.

Right now, go ahead and leave the chairs where they are from the repetition exercise. Just move locations so you are working with your scene partner. [Wait until they sit back down.] You should have your scenes memorized, so before we go ahead with today's lesson, we need to do a quick run-though of your scenes. Those lines must be fresh in your mind before we begin an activity that deals primarily with *tools*. Again, do not do line readings. Simply say the lines to each other in monotone voices. Go ahead and do that now. [Have the students run lines twice for good measure.] And, stop.

We will begin today's lesson with the '*as if* game.' Therefore, if you would, please place your attention on your partner. What you see in the moment now will determine what tool you use as you improvise your lines of the *as if*. When I say *go*, you will begin. When I say *line*, you will switch from improvising lines to the actual text of your scene. Remember to take the color of your delivery with you as you shift into using the lines of the scene. For today's lesson, though, I *want* you to pay special attention to shifting *tools* when necessary. Remember, you shift *tools* because you need a new way to achieve your *action*. You decide you need a new tactic when your partner does something that requires you to change *tools*. You make that decision based on what you see. Up to this point, I was not concerned about you shifting because you were still learning about *tools* and the game itself; however, today's lesson is about freely shifting *tools* when necessary. In addition, you can finally feel free to stand and move around from this point forward—if your body tells you to move.

What I mean by 'if your body tells you to move' has to do with instincts. If you instinctually *want* to move because it is necessary to complete your *action* and/or shift *tools*, then please do so in this lesson and future lessons. Let's give it a try. Please pay close attention to your partner. Ready, *go*. [Let the '*as if* game' pick up momentum before saying line.] Line! [Let the scenes move forward for as long as the students can remember their lines. Start again if many students had trouble with memorization, because memorization is absolutely necessary.] And, 'stop.' Ok. How did that go? [Field student responses. Some may say the experience was 'great,' while others may say it was 'awful.' We do what we can to achieve the best possible outcome.] Now ask if a pair of students would let everyone watch their scene. Are there any volunteers? [If there are none, ask a pair that is doing the best job.] Thank you for volunteering. You do not have to move in the space if you wish; we can all see you well enough from where we are sitting.

What I am going to do now is ask you to play the '*as if* game' into the scene. Shift *tools* when you think it is necessary to move toward achieving your *action*. Make sure you use *tools* sensibly. Do not shift just to shift. While you run the scene, the rest of the class is going to look for tool shifts that did happen or tool shifts that they think should have happened. In other words, we are going to provide you with our feedback after the scene. Oh yes, if you need your *tools* handout, you can refer to it. [Allow students to get the handout and come back to their seats.] We are going to note *tools* that you used and *tools* that might have come in handy.

This performance work is going to be difficult, but this is a safe place. If we do not do it right the first time, no harm done. We just try again. Do you understand? [Field their responses.] Now play the '*as if* game' into the scene. We are going to watch and give you some feedback after you are finished. Do the two of you understand that? [Field responses from the volunteers.] Go ahead and place your attention on your partner. What is true in the moment now? When I say *go*, you begin the scene using an appropriate tool based on what you see in your partner. When I say *line*, you shift into the text of the scene, but keep the appropriate tool and 'coloring' because that is required. Ready, go. [Let the scene build momentum before saying line.] *Line*! [Watch for *tools* being used. Especially note which *tools* were being used at which points in the exercise. Of course, let the scene run until the students are out of text. If there are errors, the exercise can be repeated.]

I think they deserve a round of applause. Volunteers, what were your '*action*s?' [Let them respond.] Ok, now, everyone take turns telling the volunteers what *tools* you saw them use. What *tools* did you see in that exercise? [Allow students to give direct answers to the volunteers. Responses may be surprising. They may be spot on or totally incorrect. The instructor must craft the responses accordingly and help the students see the *tools* that were actually used.] Now I will pose a more difficult question. Volunteers or audience, do you think different *tools* could have been used? If so, identify why and at what point in the scene. [Field student responses.] Thank you volunteers and audience. [If the experience was fruitful, ask another dyad to let the class watch them. If it was not, repeat the exercise with that same dyad before moving on to the discussion. I have found that I prefer repeating this process, trying it with another group, and even having the next group repeat the process. This is time consuming, but necessary for students. They need examples to be able to bridge the gap between what they are doing and what is anticipated. This is constructivism in process.]

Now, what we did was provide suggestions on how to shift *tools*. What I could have done in the middle of that exercise is shouted the name of one of our volunteers and said change *tools*. In fact, I could have even suggested the *tool* to use. I found this very distracting as an actor when my acting coaches did it to me. Suddenly, you hear this scream break your concentration and you try to fumble for the *tool* that was shouted at you. I just did not have the heart to do that to you right now. What I like to try first is to work through the exercise and see if we can suggest some appropriate *tool* shifts after we see the scene. If we do this enough, you will start to *tool* shift on your own. We are basically becoming familiar with the various *tools*, but they will change because the scenes will always change. That was the goal of today's exercise.

Now we will look at as many scenes as class allows. We can then offer the same commentary we did for our volunteers. It is import that everyone learns to perform on their own with an audience. Until this point, we have not put many people 'on the stage.' Yet, we really need to do that soon if we are going to transition from class exercise to performance. Are there any volunteers who wish to go next? [Lead the exact same exercise as class time allows. If there are no volunteers, choose the pairs one after the other.]

If you would, please move your chairs back to what we have deemed the audience section of the classroom and have a seat. [Wait for the students to do this.] We looked at many scenes and offered some great advice. [It would be ideal to see all the scenes. If time does not allow for it, this exercise can be continued in the following class meeting.] As I said, we must keep a safe environment if we are going to feel free to fail. Only through that freedom to fail are we able to risk, because we are amongst those who support us.

What we did today was work through *tool* shifting. As I said, I did not coach or direct the scenes by shouting '*tool* shift' or by suggesting a *tool* during the scene. Now, I can do that if you would like me to, but at this point I prefer our present format of peer to peer feedback. Next class we are going to talk about rehearsing scenes for performance. Review your lines and start to think about possible scenic elements for your scene. What I mean by scenic elements is not walls, windows, or doors; I mean tables, chairs, boxes, and/or some basic props. Next class we will integrate the Practical Aesthetics system with standard stage movement. You will notice I did not use the term 'blocking.' By the way, could anyone explain what blocking means? [Field responses.] I prefer to talk about stage movement simply as stage movement for two reasons. First, it is difficult to block scenes in Practical Aesthetics since movement is motivated by the actor pursuing an *action*. Second, if I were to block your scenes, it might interfere with the natural development of the scene itself. Instead, what we are going to do is explore moving in space according to our chosen *action*s and *tools*. That will help us move appropriately on stage. This is our last step before we run fully integrated Practical Aesthetics rehearsals and start to think about putting our scenes on stage. I look forward to seeing you in class." [For a constructivist analysis of this lesson, instructors should see Table 5.8.]

TABLE 5.8 "Shifting *Tools*"

Title:	Lesson M8 - "Rehearsal and Shifting *tools*" Constructivist Analysis
Subject:	Acting
Level:	I
Objectives:	The students will practice repetition, the "*as if* game," and shifting "*tools*" in pursuit of an "*action.*" The students will practice the actual lines of their scenes. The students will analyze other students' work and provide peer feedback about what "*tools*" were used and suggest others as need be. The students will begin thinking about integrating movement into their scenes.
Situation:	The students will all work with "*tools*," and how to shift "*tools*" within a scene, in order to work toward achieving an "*action.*"
Groups:	Students will work in dyads. In addition, students will also be placed in the position of peer reviewer.
Bridge:	A bridge is provided by knowing the "*as if* game" and "*tools*" in addition to watching fellow students practice shifting "*tools.*" By viewing others, the students learn how to approach their own scene work. We also reviewed several familiar terms. This type of continual review helps construct a more complex schema.
Exhibit:	The instructor will be able to evaluate each dyad as they perform for the entire class. The instructor can then comment on the proper use and shifting of "*tools.*" The instructor will also guide peer to peer critiques, so they happen in a healthy and helpful manner.
Reflection:	The instructor frequently asks the students to process their experiences. The instructor should take care to note what the students did well and what they did not do well. He/she can then give immediate feedback or feedback during the next lesson. The instructor is also finally able to see each dyad perform alone. He/she should use this opportunity to praise and also guide the students so they perform Practical Aesthetics correctly. An instructor should never allow students to do anything incorrectly. He/she should simply explain any problems and help the students work though them. This lesson provides a perfect opportunity to assess student work. It also works as a check on how well he/she is teaching the system. The instructor must correct and/or improve his/her teaching whenever necessary.
Assignment:	The students should keep practicing their lines.

lesson M9: "Rehearsal into Performance"

Lesson narrative

"Welcome back. It is time for repetition with someone other than your scene partner. [Repetition is found in Lesson M3.] Now that we are finished, please leave the chairs where they are, but move to a seat with your scene partner. Our class today is going to be very similar in format to our last class, but we are adding elements necessary for formal performance. Essentially, today's lesson presents the rehearsal process you would follow during the days or week/weeks before a scene is presented to an audience. The same process would be followed when staging a full-length play, but you would have analyzed each scene, modified *action*s according to the given beats, and determined an *overarching action* to help appropriately guide your scene by scene analyses.

An overarching *action* is simply a character's predominant *action* that encapsulates an entire play. The overarching *action* helps the actor make certain each scene analysis makes sense, each scene analysis does not violate the playwright's intentions, and each scene analysis does not violate the world of the play. I refrained from mentioning this earlier because I did not want to overwhelm you with having to worry about what may seem to be a grand and perplexing task. Now that you have learned the Practical Aesthetics system, choosing an overarching *action* for a character you portray in a full-length play will be no more intimidating than analyzing a scene for our class. Do you understand what I mean by overarching *action*? [Field student responses if there is confusion but instruct them that they may now read their full play.] If I may use a term from the world of technology, I have been trying to make Practical Aesthetics as 'user friendly' as possible. That is why we talked about scenes before tackling the overarching *action* of the entire play. Today's lesson will now proceed.

Today we are going to run one scene at a time, just as we did last class, but add needed set pieces and movement. I do not expect to see Broadway level performances in our first run. I expect to see you stumbling over chairs, turning your back to us while speaking so we cannot hear you, not knowing where to walk, and bumping into one another. Well, let's hope it is not that chaotic; I was being hyperbolic—unless the scene calls for it. I just hope you to feel comfortable to move from your head, heart, and/or gut. Listen to your instincts, of course, but do not worry about doing things 'right.' It is the moment and atmosphere for you to experiment. That is why we call it rehearsal. I hope to see where your *actions* and chosen *tools* take you.

In addition, I need to be very clear about my role during these rehearsals: I do not want to direct you. In future rehearsals I might make some staging suggestions, but I do not wish to block the scene or shout suggestions during the scene. You need to make discoveries as actors. If you are totally confused or are just being challenged I will be here for you. Nevertheless, I have to avoid meddling too much in your creative process, because you are now building your own understanding of what it is to be an actor. Are there any questions or concerns? [Field student questions.]

Now, before I ask for volunteers to go first, you should do a monotone run-through of your scenes. The monotone run-through helps with memorization and stops you from predetermining how lines will be delivered in performance. After you do that, talk briefly to your partner about your set. I need you to determine what furniture, or lack thereof, you might need or might eventually like to use. We can set the stage with what is available to us in the classroom and worry about the rest later. Go ahead and run your scenes. Then talk to your partner briefly about setting the stage. [Give the students a moment to run the scenes and discuss setting. Improvise props if necessary, but avoid miming. For example, a stapler can stand in for a phone.] We need some volunteers to go first. I know it is asking a great deal of you, but remember you are in a safe place. You may fail as much as you want as long as you are willing to get back up and try again. Are there any volunteers? [Try to get volunteers. If no one volunteers, then choose which dyad was best prepared to go first.] Thank you for volunteering. Go ahead and set the stage as you see fit and let me know when you are ready to begin. [Let the two actors set the stage, ask any questions, and get situated on stage.]

Here is how this is going to work. We are going to run the scene twice. The first time we are going to go from the '*as if* game' into the scene. The second time we are going to forgo the '*as if* game' and begin the scene with your lines. You have all come a long way this semester, so you have to drop the '*as if* game' training wheels at some point, right? That does not mean you forget about the *as if*. You keep that in mind to jump start your active pursuit of your *action*. With time, patience, and practice you will not even need to play the '*as if* game' before you perform. For now, however, we will run the scene once with the '*as if* game' and once without it. Are you ready? [I like to wait for students to provide some sort of affirmative acknowledgement before I start the scene because they are often nervous.] Please think of your *action*. [Take a pause.] Go ahead and think of your *as if*. [Again, take a pause.] Place you attention on your partner. What is true in the moment now? What tools might you use? When I say go, talk out your *as if*s. When I say line, switch to the lines of the scene. Ready, *go*. [Let the actors talk out their *as if*s for at least 45 seconds.] *Line!* [Let the scene come to its natural end.]

Thank you for your work. I *want* to go right back to the scene without discussion. This time we are going to start with the lines of the scene. Do not worry about whether the movement you just did was right or wrong. No two performances are ever the same. Let's just jump back in the scene and feel free to change any movements you wish. Go ahead and place your attention on your partner. What's true in the moment now? *Line!* [Again, let the scene come to its natural end.] How did that feel? How do you think it went? What was hard, and what was easy? Give us your thoughts. [Let the students say whatever comes to mind.] Audience, let's provide some positive comments. What did you like about the scene? [Have the students in the audience speak directly to the students on stage.] Do you have any constructive criticisms to make the scene better? [Again, have the students in the audience speak directly to the students onstage.] Let's have a round of applause. [Wait for the applause to end.] We are ready for our next volunteers. Who would like to go next? [If there are no volunteers, choose the next dyad to perform. Then repeat this exact process. The activity may have to be continued during the next class or classes so all scenes may be viewed.]

Go ahead and move all the chairs back to what we consider the audience section of the classroom and have a seat. [Wait for the students to move and be seated.] I *want* to congratulate you all because you have finally worked your way through the entire Practical Aesthetics Acting System. We will rehearse a little more before holding a dress rehearsal and showcasing these scenes, but the rehearsal process will not change. This is the process we will do whenever we do scene work. In fact, the second time you ran through your scenes today will be exactly what we do in performance. Trust me; though, things will move much faster as you become familiar with the process. In addition, we will not always watch a single pair of students perform in class. The more familiar you are with the process, the easier it will be for multiple scenes to be rehearsing concurrently. When we do that I will walk around and comment on your work. Of course, we will try to have each scene complete a practice run at some point in front of the class so we can provide feedback; however, we will not need to spend all this time watching individual scenes. This was the first time you did scene work using the Practical Aesthetics system, so we had to take our time and learn from one another.

I must say I am very proud of your work. Do we have more to learn? Sure! Actors are constantly learning; they never stop. For example, we have to become more adept at working with scenic objects and props, we have to become used to moving with other actors on stage, we have to become more confident in pursuing our *actions* and shifting *tools*, we even need to learn how to more effectively use our voices on stage. Now that we know the basic structure of Practical Aesthetics; however, achieving these other goals becomes possible. I certainly look forward to seeing you achieve these goals. For your assignment, continue to keep your lines fresh in your minds. Take care. I will see you next class." [For a constructivist analysis of this lesson, instructors should see Table 5.9.]

TABLE 5.9 "Rehearsal into Performance"

Title:	Lesson M9 - "Rehearsal into Performance" Constructivist Analysis
Subject:	Acting
Level:	I
Objectives:	The students will put the final parts of the Practical Aesthetics system together. The students will also understand the role of the "overarching *action*" in a play.
Situation:	Each student dyad will practice transition from the "*as if* game" to the scene itself. Each dyad will then practice running their scene without the "*as if* game." This is the first time the actors are called upon to rehearse in the same way they will perform in the future.
Groups:	Students will be in both dyads and a large group. They will practice the system in dyads, but then will offer compliments and constructive criticism as an audience viewing specific dyads. The class will end with a short lecture/discussion in which the students will be in a single group.
Bridge:	The students will take what they have learned from previous classes to complete the Practical Aesthetics Acting System. In addition, students will have the opportunity to view others and apply what they see to their own work. When fielding student responses, the instructor must keep in mind that each individual has both unique and shared experiences. Therefore, the instructor can draw from both to offer explanations and clarifications when necessary. Of course, an automatic bridge is also present because the process of rehearsal is strikingly similar to the process of performance. The cognitive link that draws everything together can easily be traced back to repetition. I suggest doing this verbally a number of times throughout a semester. That bridge helps with the transfer from rehearsal to performance that is often missing with the use of disjointed acting exercises. Drawing attention to that cognitive link helps students build cohesive acting schemas.
Exhibit:	The instructor and the class will view and evaluate individual dyads. The instructor should take care not to direct unless absolutely necessary. Students must have the opportunity to practice (which may lead to success or failure) without excessive instructor interference.
Reflection:	The instructor must field questions when necessary. He/she must also be sure to check student understanding of basic stage conventions in concert with Practical Aesthetics. The instructor can direct, but only if necessary, to keep students on track during rehearsal.
Assignment:	The students should keep their lines fresh in their memories.

Reference

Bruder, Melissa, et al. *A Practical Handbook for the Actor.* New York: Vintage Books, 1986. Print.

6
TRAINING THE VOICE WHILE USING PRACTICAL AESTHETICS

Practical Aesthetics does not claim its own organically created voice and diction or movement training system for the stage. Chuck Jones' *Make Your Voice Heard: An Actor's Guide to Increased Dramatic Range Through Vocal Training* and Edith Skinner, Timothy Monich, and Lilene Mansell's *Speak with Distinction: The Classic Skinner Method to Speech on the Stage* for voice/speech/diction were used. Jones drew upon Kristin Linklater's work, so Linklater techniques were also used. These texts and techniques are not new to actor training. Other systems use these texts and techniques. Nevertheless, I chose exercises that seem to fit nicely within the Practical Aesthetic system and Constructivist pedagogy. I use them today for this very reason.

Strangely, for the first seven years of my teaching career, I did not use any formal voice and movement exercises. The reason was because I was never taught these or any other specific systems until I attended the Atlantic. I simply relied on making sure actors could be seen, heard, and understood. It honestly seemed to work for me, until I discovered that my students were winging it on stage. They were not engaging the mind, voice, and body on stage; they were saying lines at one another and following my organic blocking. I just figured they were young, and I was young. I thought they might not understand. This was my mistake. It seems to me that this type of thinking often fosters the production of mediocre performance, because an instructor doubts the ability of the actors. I had a revelation: I do not think mediocre acting is linked to age. I think mediocre acting can be linked to an inexperienced instructor who misunderstands a young person's vocal, physical, and mental abilities. For example, why did I once mic my actors for an audience of 300? They did not need mics. This was roughly around the same time I started searching for new ways to teach acting and found Practical Aesthetics.

When I started using Practical Aesthetics, I still had not adopted a specific voice, diction, and movement system because I found it difficult to recreate what I had learned in New York. I knew I had to make a change, so I started looking at the various philosophies of voice and movement more closely. I began with what I was already familiar with from my studies at the Atlantic and researched those exercises. I started to study Linklater and Skinner by going back to read about what I was taught. This became very beneficial for this book. I learned that:

> The Linklater Approach is designed to liberate the natural voice rather than to develop a vocal technique. The basic assumption of the work is that everyone possesses a voice capable of expressing, through a two-to-four octave natural pitch range, whatever gamut of emotion, complexity of mood and subtlety of thought he or she experiences. The second assumption is that the tensions acquired through living in this world, as well as defenses, inhibitions and negative reactions to environmental influences, often diminish the efficiency of the natural voice to the point of distorted communication. Hence, the emphasis here is on the removal of the blocks that inhibit the human instrument as distinct from the development of a skillful musical instrument. I must underline at the outset that in our perception of our own voices there is a vital difference to be observed between what is 'natural' and what is 'familiar.'
> (*Freeing the Natural Voice* 1)

This provided me with a place to start, so I started building up a Linklater based curriculum.

I began using some of the exercises from *Freeing the Natural Voice*, within reason since Linklater believes that what hampers a successful performance is "the possible limits of talent, imagination or life experience" (2). My distillation of Practical Aesthetics denies the necessity of "talent." The assumption of "talent," whatever "talent" actually is, stalls instruction and is not at all Constructivist in nature. Ironically, Linklater is not alone in her thinking about talent. In *A Challenge for the Actor*, Uta Hagen states in the first sentence of her prologue:

> It takes talent. Talent is defined in the dictionary as 'the natural endowment of a person with special or creative aptitudes.' In an actor, I believe, these endowments consist of high sensitivity and responsiveness to sight, sound, touch, taste, and smell, of exceptional sensitivity to others, of being easily moved by beauty and pain, and of having a soaring imagination without losing control of reality (xiii).

Approaching the beginning actor and requiring "talent" before anything else seems absurd for the acting instructor. In addition, few beginning actors have a plethora of life experience. We do all have imagination; we were children once! So, I sided with David Mamet in believing hard work and dedication can produce talent. This opened my eyes to seeing how I could take pieces from different philosophies, including Linklater's, if I made sure they fit within my Constructivist pedagogy and Practical Aesthetics. Therefore, the following lessons on voice and movement are the result of this work. I personally crafted these lessons using Constructivist pedagogy to teach my students basic voice/diction and movement as part of a Practical Aesthetics based acting curriculum.

The first lesson in this section of the book is based on Linklater's relaxation and warm-up exercises. A warm-up is necessary *before* starting actor training. In addition, I briefly talk about diaphragmatic breath support, show the students how to identify their "centers," and help them find a pre-performance "neutral position." Again, I made sure these exercises were in line with Practical Aesthetics so as not to present a disjointed system.

The second lesson takes a closer look at breath control as well as the use of pitch and resonance in vocal production. In addition to Linklater work, I use some easy to understand contemporary sources for this purpose. This is a short lesson because it allows the instructor time in class to review the previous warm-up lesson or start with segments of the previous warm-up in class. Once the students become familiar with these activities, I move on to Skinner. This seems logical for actor growth; voice and support help with diction.

Skinner is interesting because she advocates a universal "stage speech" with which many theatre artists now disagree. That does not mean there are not valuable lessons to be learned in her book. When I took voice and diction it seemed to me that all an actor had to do to speak skillfully on stage is memorize Skinner's entire text, *Speak with Distinction*. Then an actor would be able to say all words correctly and be heard in all corners of the theatre. I attempted to do this when I was training at the Atlantic, but I needed flexibility when working with my students. So again, I pulled things from Skinner that did not violate Constructivism or Practical Aesthetics. Therefore, my third lesson covers Skinner's "Warm-Up Exercises and Phrases," "Challengers for the Actor with Good Speech," and the "Theatre Standard [for words using WH]" (*Speak with Distinction* 30–33, 334–335). These exercises were particularly successful for students who were unaware that an audience could not understand what they were saying because of their pronunciation. It is important to note that these voice and speech activities did exist as disjointed exercises but are integrated into my Practical Aesthetics based classroom.

My goal is to urge the instructor using this book in the classroom to allow students to become active learners when working with speech and later with movement. "According to constructivist learning theory, active learning occurs when the learner engages in appropriate cognitive processing during learning, which includes attending to relevant incoming information, mentally organizing it into a coherent cognitive structure, and mentally relating it with relevant prior knowledge from long-term memory" (Mayer 188). The mission of the instructor must be to help the student link the learning of speech, and movement, to previous experiences working with Practical Aesthetics. This way the learner realizes he/she can call upon speech and movement in future scene analyses and performances to be seen, heard, and to pursue an "action."

Therefore, the following lessons are meticulously documented to allow teachers to use the narrative text in class and to keep participants from being injured. If narrative descriptions are vague, there is a greater possibility for incorrect instruction. If physical exercises are done incorrectly, damage is possible. So, for the safety of the students and integrity of the lessons themselves, I provide detailed descriptions. Once the instructor masters the exercises and the students become comfortable, I expect the instructor to use his/her professional judgment to modify the lessons according to the needs and safety of his/her students. This also means that voice and also movement exercises from other systems can be used as long as they do not violate a Constructivist approach to Practical Aesthetics.

Lesson V1: "Warming up the vocal instrument"

Lesson narrative

"Welcome back to acting class. Today each actor will discover how to warm-up his/her vocal instrument for speech. Interestingly enough, the first step is relaxation. We will be using the Linklater approach. Find a comfortable place on the floor to lie down on your back. Now, close your eyes and picture a comfortable place that is very peaceful to you (Linklater 52). This place can be a beach, your grandmother's kitchen, a park, or any place that you feel extremely comfortable. Take a moment to visualize that place. [Give the students about a minute to do this.] Turn your attention to the tiny involuntary rise and fall of natural, relaxed breathing deep in the center of your body. Let your lips fall apart and feel the outgoing breath escape over the front of your mouth making a small 'fff' [breath] as it leaves your body [but do not create a vibrating sound] (Linklater 52). [Give the students about a few minutes to do this.] Forget about any worries that you have for this time. During this time we are studying acting, so we only want to pay attention to what we are doing in this moment. Remember that I used that same phrase when we were doing repetition exercises and learning Practical Aesthetics. Being in the moment is essential for the performer [Pause for about a minute or two.] Again, using the Linklater approach try alternating [the sound] 'huh-huh' and [the breath] 'fff' (Linklater 53). Go ahead and do that. [The instructor should demonstrate/lead by making the sound for as much time as the students.] Now that our five or six minutes of relaxation and clearing the mind is up, feel free to imagine yourself being transported from the place you imagined back to our classroom. I want you to maintain the state of relaxation as you open your eyes. Go ahead and do that. [Give them a moment to do this.] Slowly stand and come to form a circle in the center of the classroom. [Give them a moment to do this.] I have a question for you. Why do you think an actor has to be relaxed before performing? [Field student responses. Hopefully the word 'focus' enters the conversation. If it does not the instructor can ask if relaxation provides 'focus' and if acting requires 'focus.']

Having gotten to a place of relaxation, we need to get our body and our vocal instrument warmed-up for today's activity. Stand in a circle and put your right arm into the circle. Give it a shake for eight seconds. And, stop. Go ahead and put your left arm into the circle, and give it a shake for eight seconds. And, stop. Place your right leg into the circle, and give it a shake for eight seconds. And, stop. Put your left leg into the circle, and give it a shake for eight seconds. And, stop. Place both arms in the circle and give them just a quick shake for three seconds. And, stop.

While we are all facing into the circle, gently place your right ear next to your right shoulder; do not worry about trying to make them touch. Now gently place your left ear next to your left shoulder. In a clockwise manner, gently place your chin to your chest. Then gently bring your right ear to your right shoulder. Go ahead and do that ½ circle neck rotation three times. [Wait for them to complete the exercise.] Please do the exact same motion three times, but this time in a counter clockwise fashion. We protect the neck by not moving our head in large circles. Keep moving in ½ circles. And stop.

Now, please take your fingers and massage the muscles that surround your jaw-bone. [Demonstrate/lead the exercise.] Massage the muscles with enough pressure to warm them up, so they can be easily controlled during speech. [Let this continue for 15–20 seconds.] Please release the muscles of your lower jaw so your mouth almost falls open. Without knocking your teeth together, use your hands to move your lower jaw gently up and down. [Let this continue for 10 seconds.]

We should work a little more on the face muscles. Go ahead and vibrate your lips. Yes, make the sound of a boat's engine starting. Please do that three more times. [Wait for the students to complete the action.] Pucker your lips together and then pull in your lips toward your teeth to make the biggest smile you possibly can. Do that four more times. Next, raise and lower your eyebrows 10 times.

It is now time to do something a little bit different. Please make the 'biggest' face you possibly can. What I mean is, try to use as many muscles in your face as possible. You can even open your mouth as wide as possible. For many people this is a giant smile and for others it resembles a shocking look of surprise. Let me show you. [Demonstrate the activity.] It is now your turn; go ahead and do that. And, stop. Now make the 'smallest' face you possibly can. This usually looks like someone puckering his/her lips and squinting. Let me show you. [Demonstrate the activity.] Go ahead and do that. [Wait for them to complete the exercise.] Thank you. Now, make a big face again. Then, make a little face. Big face. Little face. Big face. Little face. Big face Little face. [Students may laugh at this point.] Please stop. Why did we do these exercises? [Field responses. The instructor wants the students to engage in a brief acknowledgement of the need for facial expressions on stage. Students may make this connection quickly. If not, the Constructivist educator must then ask how facial expressions can support an actor working toward achieving an action in a scene. A short discussion can commence about the role of the face in performance. The instructor can even reference the students' facial expressions from past repetition exercises (if he/she remembers) to show how the face is used for expression.]

Let us change focus and look at the body. It is important during performance work to have what I will call a 'neutral position' of the body. The 'neutral position' is a comfortable body position that allows an actor to find his/her 'center' which also allows the spine to be aligned. I will show you how to take a 'neutral position.' Face into the circle and imagine that there is a string connected to the top of your head. Take your right hand and grab hold of the string and pull it up. Put your other hand at your side, but please act as though the string is still connected. Keep imagining the string, but make sure your feet are hip width apart. Now I will show you how to find your center by using a quote from a strange source: *Ballet for Dummies*. I am not embarrassed to do so because it is an incredibly concise and descriptive way to help you find your center. According to the text, check to be sure you are supporting your mid-section by 'engaging your thigh muscles, [now] straighten your knees—but without pushing back into your knee joints ... [and] lift your abdominal muscles upward and back towards your spine' (Speck and Cisneros 48). That is your 'center.' In addition, your feet should stay hip width apart, your weight should be evenly distributed on both feet, and your shoulders should be in a relaxed position. Make sure your chest is not pointed out but relaxed, and you should be standing straight in a natural fashion. Do not stand like we are being called to attention at a military base. Also, think of the role of gravity in keeping you attached to the ground. When you pull that string from the top of your head, this 'neutral position' becomes the starting point from which the actor begins his/her work on stage. It also can be called upon by a teacher or director if he/she sees an actor slouching, keeping his/her hands in pockets, or oddly crossing his/her legs in an 'x.' Many of us do this by habit or because we are somehow trying to hide. It is odd to try and hide on stage, because there is no way you can do it. Therefore, you should have a 'neutral position' which feels comfortable, finds your 'center,' and allows your body to be available to you as a performer in pursuit of an action. You may have to get used to this position, but the basic idea is really to make you present in your body at the time of performance. Now relax for a second. We should practice going to that neutral position. Remember what it felt like?

Imagine that string and pull yourself into a 'neutral position.' I will walk around and see if you are in that position. If you are not, I will suggest how to correct your body position. Go ahead and do that. [Travel around the circle to make sure all students understand what was asked. Some may require help finding a 'neutral position.' Avoid touching the student and try to verbally explain what he/she needs to do to find a 'neutral position.'] Please continue imagining that string pulling you into a 'neutral position.'

Now, we are going to imagine cutting the string with a pair of scissors. [I learned this and the following mirror exercise at the Atlantic.] When you do this, imagine that your head falls forward and your chin is close to, but not touching, your chest. From that position, you should curl your spine down one vertebra at a time starting with your upper back until you are bending at the waist and your arms are dangling in front of you. When you get close to bending at the waist, release your weight a bit and gently fall into what you may recognize as 'rag-doll' position. Let's go ahead and try that. Cut the string. [Wait until they complete the exercise.] Since we are in 'rag-doll,' roll up one vertebra at a time starting with the lower back until we return to our 'neutral position.' Complete that action at this point. [Wait until they complete the exercise.] We are going to call this our 'spine alignment' activity. Everyone should do it again, so go ahead and imagine the string. Cut the string. [Continue talking the students through the 'spine alignment' activity until we are back at 'neutral.'] So, I have a question for you. Why did we do this activity? [Field student responses. The general reason why we do this is for preparing the body to work on stage without interference from nervous habits. Those habits can interfere with ease of movement and even how we achieve our *action*.]

There is still one area of the face that we did not exercise. That is inside the mouth. Come over to the large mirror on the wall. [Students should move relatively close to the mirror and be facing it. If the classroom is not equipped with a wall mounted mirror, students can be given hand mirrors, or even required to bring mirrors into class.] I know this is going to feel silly, but open your mouth as widely as you can and look inside. You may have to stick out your tongue a bit to see the roof of your mouth and the opening to your throat. Go ahead and do that now. For us to be prepared for the sheer amount of dialogue we use on stage, we have to make sure our mouth muscles are prepared. Therefore, as Edith Skinner states, we must limber them up. While looking in the mirror, try and make yourself yawn (Skinner 31). As you do so, look how the upper back half of the mouth raises. And, stop.

That area is what we call the 'soft palate.' The actual roof of your mouth is your 'hard palate.' You should see the opening to your throat, your tongue, and your teeth. You must know what these things look like if you are going to use them on stage.

Next, place your hands right below your breastbone. From way down inside, make the sounds 'ha-ha-hi.' Let's try it. Feel what happens in the area below your breastbone when you say 'ha-ha-hi' with as much force as you feel comfortable. Please follow me. Ready, 'ha-ha-hi.' I'd like to do that again. Ready, 'ha-ha-hi.' What did you feel with your hands? [Field student responses.] Right! That thing 'pushing-down' or 'down and out' is your diaphragm. Sound is created when the diaphragm pushes air from the lungs up through the vocal folds in your throat to hollow areas of your face and into your mouth. Those hollow spaces, your palates, tongue, and teeth help articulate that sound into speech. In order to speak with volume and control, you must learn to speak from the diaphragm like we just did. [The instructor can demonstrate this task and ask the students to do the same. I usually ask the students to tell each other what they had for dinner last night while supporting their speech with diaphragmatic breathing. It can get loud, but it shows the difference between this type of speech and speaking from the throat.]

So let us assume the sound is coming into the mouth, but our tongue is lazy or not warmed-up. That will affect our quality of speech. This affects whether we can be heard by an audience who may be sitting quite a distance from where we are performing. It also affects how we attack our *action*. Right? We want to be in the best form to use both sound and words to fight for our *action*. Therefore, let's do some tongue stretches and exercises. I know this will look and seem strange, but it is necessary.

According to the *30 Minute Voice Workout*, fold the tip of your tongue behind your top row of teeth and push your tongue out of your mouth. Go ahead and do that gently. You should feel a tongue stretch. Fold the tip of your tongue behind your lower row of teeth and push your tongue out of your mouth. Go ahead and do that gently. You should feel another type of stretch (Leigh) Now, according to Skinner, stick your tongue out as far (but as comfortably) as you can. In a clockwise fashion and then in a counter clockwise fashion move your tongue in circles three times (Skinner 31). These stretches allow us to be able to use our tongue to form words and control articulation. You can relax for a moment but remain looking in the mirror.

I know it may feel strange to stare at a mirror and do these things, but it is important for each one of us to examine his/her vocal instrument and understand what is happening to make sound. Only then can we be comfortable with what is inside our mouth. That allows us to then understand how we form words from sounds. Of course we do it naturally, but you now see the things that go into making speech. We must always try to be heard and understood while on stage. In addition, being able to control our voice and speech is useful for achieving an *action*. How can controlling your voice and speech be useful for achieving an *action*? [Field student responses. The students may understand that pitch, tone, volume, etc. all color our speech. If not, the instructor must help. He/she may state that how we color our speech can affect how successful we are at achieving an *action*. For example, quiet reasoning may be better in some situations while bombastic screaming might be better in another. Draw the students as close to this understanding as possible.] Please go back to the circle.

A final way we can clarify our voice is to 'shake it into place.' We are going to do this by way of something called the 'humming series.' I learned this exercise at the Atlantic Theatre in New York. It was explained to me that the 'humming series' allows the voice to settle into its natural position. If we do not do the 'humming series,' we can speak in the wrong register. So, let's go ahead and 'shake our voice into place.' Now hum along with me at three different pitches. The first one will be the lowest pitch, the second will be a little higher, and the third will be highest. Let's practice just the pitches on a 'hum.' Ready, go. ['Hum' three ascending pitches and make sure the students follow.] Now, we are going to add bodily movement and open our mouths. So, on the first pitch everyone should start humming. We are then going to open our mouths while we quickly raise and lower our shoulders. That will turn the sound from a 'hum' to an 'ahhh.' Let's practice that. [The instructor makes the lowest pitch hum, raises and lowers his/her shoulders, and opens his/her mouth to form a shaking 'ahhh.' The students should follow. If they do not, repeat the exercise.] On the second pitch we will do the same thing, but instead of raising and lowering the shoulders we will open our mouths and bounce our body on our knees. I will model the instructions and then we will do it together. Finally, on the third and highest pitch we will open our mouths to allow the 'hum' to become 'ahhh' and we will gently jump. I will model the activity and then we will do it together. Finally, we will complete the whole series once or twice more. [The instructor and students complete the exercise.]

You should notice that my voice is crisper and clearer. There is no 'frog' in my throat, and my voice is in the right register. [This is what usually happens to me when I complete this exercise.] See if that is true of your voice, too. I will pair you up into a dyad. [The instructor walks around and just points to two people standing next to each other, so they form a dyad.] Will one of you turn to your partner and tell him/her what you have planned for lunch or dinner today? If you have nothing planned, just tell them what you might like to eat today. When you are finished, let the other person say the same. Go ahead and do that now. [Sometimes the students notice a difference right away and sometimes they do not. There is time for practice and listening in the future, so I am not overly concerned with making them immediately hear something different; however, it is always nice if they do discover something.] Ok, great! I know this was an involved lesson, but the warm-up itself moves much more quickly once we memorize it. Go ahead and have a seat in the audience area so we can talk about what we did today.

Today I led you through a series of exercises to warm-up the vocal instrument. In your own words, please tell me why we actors should bother doing this? [Field student responses. They are usually savvy about why warm-ups are necessary. What they often do not consider is the use of speech sounds to support an actor's pursuit of an action. Therefore, the instructor must coax them along a bit to get that information. Once they make the connection, however, the instructor can ask a truly Constructivist question.] 'When in the last few class periods do you think the warm-up might have helped you work though our Practical Aesthetics exercises?' [Field student responses.]

Ok, we have just enough time left for a few rounds of repetition; I do not want you to forget how to do it. You can move your chairs if you like, but we must remember to move them back at the end of class. Please go ahead and pair up with someone you have not worked with before. Move your chairs. [Give the students time to do this.] It is time to practice repetition. Place your attention on your partner. As I have repeatedly said in the M3 Lesson on repetition 'what's true in the moment now?' Ready, go. [Let the repetition go on for a few minutes and repeat the exercise if there is time.] And, stop.

Thank you for your work today! We have accomplished a great deal. If you moved your chair, go ahead and put it back in what we consider the audience section. [Wait for them to do so.] For homework, continue learning the lines from your current scene; however, make sure you do not practice how to say the lines. DO NOT ACT. Just memorize them in a monotone voice. Are there any questions before class is over? [Answer any student questions.] Are there any questions about what we did in class today? [Field any questions.] Just to check, I would like one or two people to verbalize why we did one of today's warm-up activities. [Field student responses as time allows. I have had students argue about the need for warm-ups, so be prepared to form an analogy using warm-ups for musicians or sports celebrities.] After we run through the entire warm-up over the next few days, I will ask one of you to take over leading the warm-up. We eventually will work through having as many students as we can lead the exercise. This allows each student to remember, verbalize, and do what needs to be accomplished in a Constructivist way. This is a very important learning tool, and we must all take it seriously. Of course, I am not going to get upset if you miss elements. I expect your classmates to help you work though each element until everything becomes second nature. I'll see you next class."

[For a constructivist analysis of this lesson, instructors should see Table 6.1.]

TABLE 6.1 "Warming Up the Vocal Instrument"

Title:	Lesson V1 - "Warming Up the Vocal instrument" Constructivist Analysis
Subject:	Acting
Level:	I
Objectives:	The students will begin to build a basic vocal instrument warm-up series for use before performance. They will infer why a warm-up is necessary. Each student will practice facial muscle exercises and become comfortable with the working of his/her voice, speech, and basic articulators. The students will elaborate on why actors need a "neutral position." The students will test diaphragmatic speech support. The students will perceive the value of the "humming series" by listening to other students after the exercise.
Situation:	Students will practice a pre-performance vocal instrument warm-up. Students are asked to process, remember, and eventually recreate an entire vocal warm-up activity for performance in future lessons.
Groups:	Students will work in a large circle. They will then work individually with a mirror. In addition, I will work one on one with a student to develop the best "neutral position" for each actor. The students will also be in dyads for testing the purpose of the "humming series" and for practicing repetition.
Bridge:	The students must identify parts of their own face and mouth. The students are also asked how voice may have affected previous performances. In the future, students will lead the warm-up. This requires the student to bridge the learning gap between application and synthesis. The students may discover a different order of exercises, but the instructor must then ask why the student chose that order. There may be a newly created valid reason (which is always exciting to discover).
Exhibit:	The instructor will view and evaluate all student activities. The instructor must feel comfortable guiding each individual student to his/her own best posture and best warm-up program. This task must be completed over time, not in one class period; however, the task begins today.
Reflection:	There is ample opportunity in this lesson for the instructor to check for understanding. If understanding is weak, the instructor must modify his/her instruction in order to adapt to the specific needs of each student. He/she must not be discouraged if errors are made in instruction. The key is to correct them, and lead the students toward active learning.
Assignment:	The students are asked to keep learning the lines of their scenes in a monotone voice.

Lesson V2: "Examining breath, resonance, and pitch"

Lesson narrative

I suggest using the vocal instrument warm-up as the warm-up to this lesson. Then complete this lesson and end with playing the '*as if* game.' This lesson is shorter, 30–45 minutes, because I am accounting for the vocal instrument warm-up and practice with the '*as if* game.'

"It's good to see everyone again. In today's class we want to talk about breath, resonance, and pitch. First, it is important to talk about breath. We need to have enough breath to manufacture sound, so grab a textbook or any book from my shelf and please lie on the floor like we did for the relaxation exercises, but this time raise your knees so you can keep your feet on the floor. [Let the students take that position.] The following exercise, which increases the amount of breath you have to convert to sound, is from Audrey June Hunt, a vocal coach from California. We will do each activity when I pause while reading the instructions:

> Simply follow your breathing for a minute or two with your attention ... [Next] Put your hands (one on top of the other) on your belly, with the center of your lower hand touching your navel. Watch how your breathing responds. You may notice that your belly wants to expand as you inhale and retract as you exhale. Let this happen, but don't try to force it ... [Now, position the] book on the belly in place of the hands. This adds weight and aids in a more pronounced feeling as you inhale. With the weight of the book resting on your belly, lift the book as you inhale and hold it for about 5 seconds. Then lower the book slowly as you exhale all of your air. Repeat, 5 or 6 times, breathing through the nose. Repeat this exercise, but this time replace just holding the book for 5 seconds with singing the numbers, 12345678910. Lower the book as you sing. [Pause.] Repeat the above exercise and increase your singing to the number 15. [Pause.] Repeat again, singing to 20 or as far as you can. DO NOT STRAIN [*sic*]. (vocalcoach.hubpages.com)

This exercise strengthens your diaphragm and develops your lung capacity. When on stage we need both to support our speech. You must practice this at home each night. This exercise will increase your lung volume so you can have increased control over your speech on stage. Go ahead and stand up; then form a circle in the center of the room. [Wait for the students to do this.] Why should you bother to increase your ability to control your speech? [Field student responses.]

At this point we must turn our attention to resonance. According to the American Academy of Otolaryngology (ear, nose, and throat doctors):

> By themselves, the vocal folds produce a noise that sounds like simple buzzing, much like the mouthpiece on a trumpet. All of the structure above the folds, including the throat, nose, and mouth, are part of the resonator system. We can compare these structures to those of a horn or trumpet. The buzzing sound created by vocal fold vibration is changed by the shape of the resonator tract to produce our unique human sound. (www.entnet.org)

Essentially, sound bounces around in the throat, nose/sinuses, and mouth before it is modified by articulators such as the soft palate, teeth, and tongue to produce speech. As actors, we can control where that sound is modified. We can decide to let it bounce around in our throat, nose/sinuses, and/or mouth to modify what we sound like. According to *A 30 Minute Voice Workout for the Actor*, one can identify your resonators by doing the following exercises. To discover your nasal and sinus resonators, place your hands on your nose and under your eyes. Now make a 'hmmm?' sound like you are suddenly surprised by what someone said. Go ahead and do that three times. Ready, *go*. [Wait for them to finish.] Did you feel the vibration? Place your fingers on your lips. We can feel our mouth as a resonator when we simply hum. Go ahead and hum for a few seconds. Ready, *go*. [Wait for them to finish.] Did you feel the vibration? Finally, place your fingers on your throat. Go ahead and say 'huh' three times. Ready, *go* [Wait for them to finish.] Those are your resonators (Leigh). I have a question for you all. Why, as actors, should you personally care about your resonators? [Field responses from students. Hopefully they are able to say that the resonators control expression. This means that sending the sound to the correct resonator can express a sound or line in a different way. The varied expression can have varied meaning. The instructor will probably have to guide them toward considering what this means when pursuing an *action*. The various meanings of expression can be used to flavor the approach an actor takes when pursuing an action.]

It is now time to talk about pitch. What does pitch have to do with an actor? [Field responses from students. Because this is being discussed right after resonators, students usually understand that pitch can have similar effects. Therefore, pitch can be used by the actor to add a specific color to the sounds he/she makes or the approach he/she takes when pursuing an action.] Let's practice various pitches. According to *A 30 Minute Voice Workout for the Actor*, go ahead and say 'ha-ha-hum' with me at various pitches. We will start low and gradually increase. Ready, follow me. [Say 'ha-ha-hum' and increase pitch as high as possible.] Let's do the same thing by vibrating our lips as we say 'BrOOm-ahh' in increasing pitches. Ready, follow me. [Say 'BrOOm-ahh' in increasing pitches as high as I can go.]

Let us change the phrasing. On a pitch following me please say, 'mi-mi-mi-mi—may-may-may-may—ma-ahhhh?' The 'ahhhh' should swing up a few pitches like a question. Say it like this. [Demonstrate to the class.] Go ahead and say it with me. Ready, go. [Lead the students in saying 'mi-mi-mi-mi—may-may-may-may—ma-ahhhh.'] And, stop. This time say on a pitch following me, 'mi-mi-mi-mi—may-may-may-may—myyyy?' The 'myyyy' should swing up a few pitches as in a question (Leigh). Say it like this. [Demonstrate to the class.] Now say it with me. Ready, *go*. [Lead the students in saying 'mi-mi-mi-mi—may-may-may-may—myyyy.'] Finally, we are going do the same thing using the phrase 'key-ee,' but the 'ee' will swing up several pitches (Leigh). I will start the first 'key-ee' at a lower pitch and gradually increase but remember that the 'ee' will swing up several pitches. Say it like this. [Demonstrate to the class.] Please say it with me. Ready, *go*. [Lead the students as before.] And, stop.

So, in this lesson, what have you learned about warm-ups, breath, resonance, and pitch? [Field responses.] The exercises we did are warm-ups, but they also show you the range at which you can use your voice. I hope you are starting to see why I think of the actor's voice as a tool for performance. He/she can always use it to add extra color to words and phrases. That extra color can mean a great deal when striving for an *action*. For example, the pitch of a word can indicate how important you think something is. When I say go, say 'hey' at a very low pitch. Ready, *go*. [The students will say 'hey.'] When I say go, you should say 'hey' at a very high pitch. Ready, *go*. [The students will say 'hey.'] Do you hear the difference? What difference does the sound make? [Field student responses.]

Before we end class, we need to review the '*as if* game' from the scenes you analyzed. Each of you find a chair and sit down with your scene partner. Please do that. [Wait for the students to take their places.] Take a moment to remember your actions and as ifs. We are going to talk out the as ifs in the '*as if* game.' Go ahead and complete the '*as if* game' when I say go. Ready, *go*. [The students do.] And, *stop*. Go ahead and complete one final round of 'the *as if* game' when I say go. Ready, *go*. [The students do.] Thank you. Go ahead and take your chairs back to our audience section of the room and have a seat. [Wait for the students to do that.] Again, thanks for all for your work today. Can anyone think of a situation from previous classes where better control of breath, resonators, and/or pitch could have been useful? [Field answers and make suggestions based on what they remember from previous classes.] Are there any questions [Field student questions.] For homework tonight, keep running your lines from your scenes. I will see you next class." [For a constructivist analysis of this lesson, instructors should see Table 6.2.]

TABLE 6.2 "Examining Breath, Resonance, and Pitch"

Title:	Lesson V2 - "Examining Breath, Resonance, and Pitch" Constructivist Analysis
Subject:	Acting
Level:	I
Objectives:	The students will experiment with more vocal warm-ups. The students will use one specific way to strengthen their diaphragm and increase lung capacity to make speech easier on stage. The students will learn about their resonators. The students will theorize about the point and purpose of resonators. The students will practice exercises devoted to pitch so they can eventually determine how to add color to specific sounds, words, and phrases using pitch.
Situation:	The students will work individually to become better acquainted with parts of the body that are used to create voice and speech.
Groups:	For the majority of the class, the students will work independently yet under the direct supervision of the instructor. For the last portion of the class, students will practice repetition in a dyad.
Bridge:	The students will explain why they should personally care about breath, resonators, and pitch. They are also asked to think of a situation from previous classes where better control of breath, resonators, and/or pitch would have been useful. In addition, their journal writing provides a bridge (in a different medium) to a student's present thoughts and past experiences. Journals can actually be assigned throughout the entire course to check on understanding.
Exhibit:	Students will demonstrate, both verbally and kinesthetically, what they have learned about warm-ups, breath, resonance, and pitch.
Reflection:	The instructor asks the students to verbalize what they did in class and why they did it. This will check student learning and allow the instructor to determine how effective his/her instruction was (for future modification).
Assignment:	The students are supposed to continue learning their lines, practice the breathing exercise learned today, and journal about breathing, resonance, and pitch.

Lesson V3: "Articulation and tongue twisters"

Lesson narrative

I suggest reviewing Lessons V/B 1 and V/B 2 as a warm-up for this lesson. These three lessons, when combined, form the "Voice/Speech" section of the system. If the class runs long, continue with this lesson during the next class period. The students need constant review and practice; constantly overwhelming them with new information will not make them better actors (quite the contrary). Simply pick up by reviewing what was covered in the previous class, add new material, and then close by reviewing material covered earlier in the course

"Please form a circle standing in the center of the room. [Wait for them to do this.] We are now going to discuss pronunciation and articulation. When on stage, there are several articulation and pronunciation difficulties that can pose a challenge to the actor. Today, I will introduce you to a few of these challenges in hopes of clarifying your speech when you act. Since this is an introduction to Practical Aesthetics for the classroom, I am not trying to turn you into what many in the theatre call a 'classical actor' or a 'Shakespearean actor.' That type of training is out of scope for this level of work. Instead, I have chosen to focus on some of the major pronunciation and articulation problems I have discovered in the approximately thirty full length plays I have directed.

Unless otherwise noted, the majority of the following exercises were taken from Edith Skinner's *Speak with Distinction*. Skinner was a very famous voice and speech coach, and her students have continued her work by adding more exercises to the text. I am simply using these exercises to help you be heard and understood on stage; I am not using these exercises to fix accents or make you sound like someone you are not.

When on stage, a beginning actor may not pronounce Ms, Ns, Ls, Ts, Ps, Ds, Ss and the two letter combination WH in a way audiences can easily understand. Because of this, we are going to do a few exercises that will help us reinforce the habit of saying these sounds clearly on stage. This exercise from *Speak with Distinction* is called 'Edith's Favorite.' Please repeat after me when I pause at the end of each line. Here we go. 'MAH MAY MEE MY MOH MOO.' [Pause for the students to repeat.] 'NAH NAY NEE NIGH NOH NOO.' [Pause for the students to repeat.] 'LAH LAY LEE LIE LOH LOO.' [The students repeat.] We will add another series. This time stress the syllables I do in the following exercises. [Stress the underlined syllables as an example.] 'MAH may me MY moh moo MAH may me MY moh moo.' [Pause for the students to repeat.] 'NAH may nee NIGH noh noo NAH nay nee NIGH noh noo.' [Pause for the students to repeat.] 'LAH lay lee LIE loh loo LAH lay lee LIE loh loo' (32). [Pause for the students to repeat. The instructor can repeat this exercise, and the following exercises, as many times as needed.]

In our next exercise we will practice saying Ps, Ts, and Ds, in addition to Ss that should make a Z sound at the end of words. We want to practice saying Ps because actors often over-aspirate them. They *are* aspirated (meaning air comes out of our mouth after we say them), but we do not want to sound like we are spitting. When it comes to Ts and Ds, actors sometimes forget to pronounce them at all. As for Ss, they can sound strange to an audience because actors sometimes like to hold the S sound so long that it sounds like a leaky tire or steam escaping. In addition, it is often the case that Ss at the end of words such as 'zippers' should sound like Z instead of S. Practicing these letters is important. It is my hope that practicing them often will cause you all to pay closer attention to the way you say them in your personal life and on stage. Yes, I said your personal life because, frankly, it is difficult to turn pronunciation off and on. Therefore, please repeat the following practice phrases from *Speak with Distinction*:

> Peter Piper the pickled pepper picker picked a peck of pickled peppers. [Students repeat.]
> A peck of pickled peppers did Peter Piper the pickled pepper picker pick. [Students repeat.] Now if Peter Piper the pickled pepper picker picked a peck of pickled peppers, [Students repeat.] Where is the peck of pickled peppers that Peter Piper the pickled pepper picker picked? [Students repeat. It is suggested to repeat this entire exercise at least twice more.] (33)

Thank you. Let's move on.

In this lesson we will be practicing Ws and the letter combination WH. Sometimes actors pronounce Ws and the WH combination the same way. Instead, the WH combination is often voiced; it does not sound like a single W. In *Speak with Distinction*, Edith Skinner suggests that 'when' is pronounced 'WHen' rather than 'Wen' (335). The reason for this is so the audience can tell the different between words that use a single W and those that use the WH combination. If actors do not do this, meaning can be lost. *According to a 30 Minute Voice Workout for the Actor*, the following exercise is helpful in making the distinction:

> Whether the weather be fair, [students repeat.] or whether the weather be not, [students repeat], whether the weather be cold, [students repeat], or whether the weather be hot, [students repeat], we'll weather the weather whatever the weather, whether we like it or not. [students repeat.] (Leigh)

Thank you. Let's move on.

Please think of the letter combination 'str' as in 'street' and 'tr' as in 'tree.' In what seems to me to be within the last few years, beginning actors have been pronouncing 'str' with an added 'h' so the word becomes 'shtreet.' Similarly, beginning actors have been pronouncing 'tr' using the 'ch' sound found in the word 'chew.' This causes the word 'tree' to become 'chree.' Since I have personally noticed this type of pronunciation, I have written my own exercise to help you avoid the 'sht' sound in words like 'street' and the 'ch' sound in words like 'tree.' We need to practice these exercises right away. Please repeat the following phrases after me: straight trees grow on the sides of the straight street near the trash trucks. [Students repeat.] What might happen if Sheila removes the straight trees from the straight street? [Students repeat.] There would no longer be straight trees stretching down the straight street, [students repeat] and the trash trucks would be stressed by the sun's trying heat. [Students repeat, and this exercise should be repeated twice more; it is rather difficult.] Let's move on.

Finally, we will practice some articulation exercises. These should also be used as a warm-up before going on stage. This time I will say a word combination, and then all of us will say that word combination repeatedly for several seconds. These phrases came from Edith Skinner's *Speak with Distinction*:

> kinky cookie [students repeat several times] … philological ability [students repeat several times] … eleven benevolent elephants [students repeat several times] … Topeka Bodega [students repeat several times] … red leather yellow leather [students repeat several times] … unique New York [students repeat several times] … toy boat [students repeat several times] … sushi chef [students repeat several times] … garlic gargle, gargle with garlic [students repeat several times] … (34–35)

Go ahead and have a seat in our audience section of the classroom. [Wait for them to become settled.] Today we practiced effective pronunciation and clear articulation. Effective pronunciation and clear articulation help an audience hear us correctly, but they also help us perform effectively as actors. For example, if we are lazy about our speech, it may seem like we are not that interested in pursuing our *action*. Remember, pursuing your *action* is essential to a solid performance.

Before class is over, tell me what you learned today. Did you learn anything new today about speech and articulation? [Field student responses.] Why must actors practice articulation before going on stage? [Field student responses.] During our past exercises, or if you have been on stage before, would better articulation have helped you in any way? [Field student responses.] Are there any questions about what we covered today? [Field student responses.] I eventually will expect you to use these voice exercises, as well as the movement exercises to come, as personal training techniques and warm-up exercises. You should practice these exercises regularly at home, and you should always warm-up before performances. If you stay involved in theatre, as I hope you will for a long time, you will eventually build an entire repertoire of these activities. For your assignment tonight, practice as many of the warm-up exercises as possible and continue learning your lines. Remember to learn your lines in a monotone voice; do not practice 'line readings.' I enjoyed working with you today. I will see you next class." [For a constructivist analysis of this lesson, instructors should see Table 6.3.]

TABLE 6.3 "Articulation and Tongue Twisters"

Title:	Lesson V3 - "Articulation and Tongue Twisters" Constructivist Analysis
Subject:	Acting
Level:	I
Objectives:	The students will review vocal warm-up exercises. The students will continue strengthening their breathing. The students will review resonator and pitch exercises. The students will apply what they learned about articulation to their theatre work. The students will start to deduce why articulation is so important for the actor.
Situation:	The students will practice (in order to improve) their stage pronunciation of the consonants M, N, L, T, P, D, S, W, and the two letter combination WH. They will also practice general articulation for the stage.
Groups:	For the majority of the class, the students will work on their own pronunciation and articulation. Yet, they are also under the direct supervision of the instructor. Therefore, the instructor should never feel bad telling students what they could do more effectively. If time permits, students will practice repetition in a dyad.
Bridge:	The students will explain why they should personally care about pronunciation and articulation. Their journal writing also provides a bridge which links past experiences to current knowledge construction.
Exhibit:	Each student will be asked to practice his/her articulation for the stage. The instructor can verbally evaluate the pronunciation of the group as well as the enunciation of the individual. The instructor should feel comfortable providing immediate feedback to the students.
Reflection:	The instructor asks the students to verbalize what they did in class and why they did it. The instructor also asks the students how articulation could have helped them in the past. This will check student learning and allow the instructor to determine how effective his/her instruction was (for future modification).
Assignment:	The students are to continue learning their lines, practice their breathing exercise, and journal about warming-up, articulation, and tongue twisters.

I suggest assigning a journal entry about today's class. The journal entry should be one half to one full page about warming-up, articulation, and tongue twisters. The students may discuss what we did in class today, but they should also focus on 'why' we did what we did today. This provides a Constructivist bridge between what was covered in class and the student's individual thoughts and/or past experiences.

An alternate homework assignment using technology might be to provide the students with a handout of today's articulation exercises. Ask them to go home and record themselves talking through the articulation exercises. They could do this via their home computer's microphone and bring in a flash drive recording for the instructor to review and/or grade. I think it interesting to comment on the recording and ask the student to review the recording after viewing the instructor's comments. It may help them hear, in their own voices, why articulation is important, especially if they doubt the need for any pronunciation and/or articulation improvement.

Works cited

Academy of Otolaryngology - Head and Neck SurgeryHow the Voice Works." 2013. Web. November 23, 2013. www.entnet.org/healthinformation/ howvoiceworks.cfm.

Hagen, Uta. *A Challenge for the Actor*. New York: Scribner's, 1991. Print.

Jones, Chuck. *Make Your Voice Heard: An Actor's Guide to Increased Dramatic Range through Vocal Training*. New York: Back Stage Books, 2005. Print.

Leigh, Susan. *A 30 Minute Voice Workout for the Actor*. Leucadia, CA: Theatre Arts Video Library, 1988. VHS.

Linklater, Kristin. *Freeing the Natural Voice*. New York: Drama Book Specialists, 1976. Print.

Hunt, Audrey. "Audrey Hunt—Vocal Coach." 2014. Web. February 2, 2014. https://hubpages.com/@vocalcoach.

Mayer, Richard E. "Constructivism as a Theory of Learning versus Constructivism as a Prescription for Instruction." *Constructivist Instruction: Success or Failure?* Eds. Sigmund Tobias and Thomas M. Duffy. New York: Routledge, 2009. Print.

Skinner, Edith, Timothy Monich, and Lilene Mansell. *Speak with Distinction*. New York: Applause Theatre Book Publishers, 1990. Print.

Speck, Scott and Evelyn Cisneros. "Finding the Correct *Ballet* Stance." *Ballet for Dummies*. Indianapolis: Wiley Publishing, Inc., 2003. Print.

7
TRAINING THE BODY WHILE USING PRACTICAL AESTHETICS

This chapter dealing with movement on stage is grounded on yoga-based exercises, those of Rudolph Laban, and Viewpoints. I learned these movement techniques while training as an actor dedicated to the Practical Aesthetics system. Again, the key point to remember is that these exercises utilize Constructivist pedagogy (e.g., they are always student focused no matter the skill of the actor) and they do not violate Practical Aesthetics. Quite the opposite. These movement exercises were specifically chosen to support the engagement of the body within Practical Aesthetics.

The first lesson focuses primarily on yoga-based exercises devoted to stretching, muscle coordination, breath support, strengthening the core, and presence. I was originally exposed to most of these exercises by my Laban instructor Renee Redding-Jones at the Atlantic Theatre Acting School, but I also rediscovered many of them in *Actor Training the Laban Way: An Integrated Approach to Voice, Speech, and Movement* by Barbara Adrian. I will reference the Adrian text, so readers can learn more about these exercises if they wish. Only the last exercise in lesson four on "presence" did I create myself. I considered it a fitting exercise to close the individual actor training methodology presented in this book before looking briefly at ensemble work.

In the second lesson I introduce ensemble work. I start with a Laban based exercise on kinesphere which can be loosely defined as an individual's personal space beyond the body. Again, I learned this exercise from Renee Redding-Jones at the Atlantic but use it specifically to lead into ensemble work. An introduction to kinesphere can help the students function well in an ensemble. The ensemble exercises that follow are derived from Viewpoints and were taught by Kelly Maurer at the Atlantic. Any instructor interested in Viewpoints will find *The Viewpoints Book* by Anne Bogart and Tina Landau extremely helpful.

I then conclude this chapter by providing a third lesson on improvisation to illustrate how improvisation can be used to teach movement. Students often believe the purpose of improvisation is to learn what to do if one forgets a line on stage or "wants to be funny." Certainly, it develops spontaneity and it can be funny; however, I use improvisation primarily to show the actor that at its core Practical Aesthetics is highly skilled improvisation—essentially "always having an *action* and being in the moment." Therefore, improvisation must be covered by the instructor who wishes to teach Practical Aesthetics.

Before I move on to the following lessons, I argue that any professionally codified and widely used movement and/or speech system has its merits. One could possibly do a study arguing for the benefits of one system over the other by how each system fares in a series of tests, but that is out of the scope of this text. I chose my movement and speech work because each works well with my Constructivist approach to Practical Aesthetics, and I believe teaching with an active Constructivist pedagogy enhances student learning. In addition, if I had to provide a key reason why I use these specific activities in these lessons, it would be because these speech and movement exercises help the acting instructor at the secondary and college level teach the actor how to achieve his/her *action*. That makes them compatible with Practical Aesthetics. Famous voice instructor Cecily Barry, Voice Director for the Royal Shakespeare Company for more than 35 years, summarizes this concept nicely. She states:

> I became deeply aware of the physical connections between the making of the word and the emotional motive of the actor—in the terms of Stanislavski, the want/need of the character in the scene. I then began to realize that the work [of the voice or speech] had to be in two parts: 1. the technical facility, and 2. how this technical facility reached into, and fused with, the actor's intentions. This has far-reaching consequences in that it could affect the presentation of the character. (Hampton and Acker, *The Vocal Vision* 25–26)

Although she is not using terminology from Practical Aesthetics, the base meaning is applicable: movement and speech are tools for the actor to achieve each *action*. It is my job as a Constructivist acting instructor to help every actor use his/her body and voice to achieve that *action* on stage. The Atlantic Theatre Acting School did the same thing by aligning themselves with Jones, Skinner, Laban, yoga, and Viewpoints. It should be mentioned that the Atlantic also used Suzuki exercises to train me and my classmates. Suzuki based work is purposely absent from this book for safety reasons. In a beginning class, I believe this is wise unless the instructor is specially trained in Suzuki methodology.

Lesson B1: "Breathing, stretching, and strengthening"

Lesson narrative

"Today we are going to practice breathing and train the body for performance by learning some Laban movement techniques for the stage. The following exercises are going to serve three purposes. The first purpose is to strengthen breathing so you have enough air in your lungs to accommodate your voice on stage; the second purpose is to strengthen the body's core, which will provide breath support for your vocal instrument; and the third purpose is to get you better acquainted with the various muscles of your body. You may be thinking to yourself that you already are well acquainted with the muscles in your body, but I have a feeling you might be surprised. Beginning actors often underestimate how physically draining a performance can be. While a short scene might not require a great deal of physical prowess, a full-length play or musical requires a great deal. Therefore, just as an athlete must prepare his/her body for a sporting event, an actor must prepare his/her body to successfully handle the demands of the stage. This does not mean it is time to learn how to run a four-minute mile or train for a marathon, but it is time to practice physical coordination. According to Barbara Adrian, a professional Laban movement practitioner, Laban movement provides 'a support for actors to know who they are as movers, [to] expand their movement potential, and [to] become their most expressive and imaginative selves' ("An Introduction" 84).

Please have a seat in your own space on the floor. Go ahead and lie back extending your hands over your head until your wrists touch the floor. Adrian requests that actors extend your legs so your legs and heels are in contact with the floor. Make sure there is an arm's length between you and anyone else around you. [Wait for the students to do this.] Let's begin. Give yourself a 'heel rock' by pressing your heels against the floor while alternating pointing your toes toward you and then away from you several times. Essentially, you will slightly pull your body back and forth (just a couple inches or so) on the floor. Let's do that several times (*Actor Training* 46). This is simply a relaxation exercise. [Let them heel rock for 30–40 seconds.] And, stop.

Now use your arms and your legs to form an 'X' on the floor with your entire body. Go ahead and give yourself a 'heel rock' with your right heel. [Let them heel rock for 30 seconds.] Give yourself a 'heel rock' with your left heel. [Let them heel rock for 30 seconds.] Now, slide your right arm and your right leg toward each other on the floor, but do not try to make them touch. And, hold. [Let them hold for 5–10 seconds.] Please go back to 'X.' At this point, slide your left elbow toward your left knee, but do not try to make them touch. And, hold. [Let them hold for 5–10 seconds.] Go back to 'X.' I would like everyone do the right side again. And, hold. [Let them hold for 5–10 seconds.] Let's do the left side again. And, hold. [Let them hold for 5–10 seconds.] Go back to 'X.' What we are doing is strengthening the muscles around our core. That exercise actually requires you to engage the muscles in your midsection.

We are now going to do some abdominal stretches. Go ahead and get into the fetal position on your right side. [Let them hold for 10–15 seconds.] Staying on your right side, slide your arms over your head and straighten your legs. It is almost like you are flying like Superman but on your right side. [Let them hold for 10 seconds.] Go back to the fetal position on your right side. [Let them hold for 10–15 seconds.] Then, go back to the 'X.' Let's go ahead and do the other side. If you would, go ahead and get into the fetal position on your left side. [Let them hold for 10–15 seconds.] This time staying on your left side, slide your arms over your head and straighten your legs. It is almost like you are flying like Superman but on your left side. [Let them hold for 10 seconds.] Go back to the fetal position on your left side. [Let them hold for 10–15 seconds.] Then, go back to the 'X.'

Now place your feet flat on the floor with your knees up, and place your hands on your waist near your belly button. Go ahead and tighten your abs, then lift your right foot a few inches off the ground and hold it there for five seconds. Put your right foot back on the ground. This time lift your left foot a few inches off the ground and hold it there for five seconds. Please put your right foot back on the ground. Do those same two lifts two more times. Ready, go. [Wait for the students to complete the exercise.] This time place the soles of your feet together and let your knees fall out to the sides. This lifting exercise strengthens your abs, or your core, and putting the soles of your feet together and letting your knees fall out to the sides is a stretch. Go ahead and stay in that stretch for about 10 seconds. [Wait for the students to stretch.]

Now place your feet flat on the floor again with your knees again pointed up. Go ahead and do that now. Tighten your abs and lift your right leg a few inches off the ground. Hold it there and lift your left leg a few inches off the ground. Keep both of your feet elevated like that for three seconds. This is another exercise that tones your core. Do that same lift of both your feet two more times. Remember to hold each lift for three seconds. Do the best that you can, because we all are different. Ready, *go*. [Lead the students in the exercise.] Put the soles of your feet together and let your knees fall out to the sides. Go ahead and stay in that stretch for about 10 seconds. [Wait for the students to stretch.] If you are having trouble with any of these exercises, do not worry. You simply need more practice. Then it will become habitual, as Practical Aesthetics requires. Practical Aesthetics does not require instantaneous 'talent' for progression. Habit is the key to perfecting the exercise.

For our next group of exercises, Adrian suggests kneeling on the floor and enter what yoga instructors call 'child's pose.' While you are kneeling, please sit back on your feet, lower your face near the floor, and extend your hands on the floor as far as you can reach. Just remain there in a stretch for about ten seconds. Please focus on your breathing. With a deep breath, try to 'expand your back with breath.' What I mean is 'expand your rib cage with breath,' but this particular exercise will allow you to feel how your whole center feels when filled with breath. Go ahead and do that. Now exhale and just focus on your normal breathing pattern. Remember that your whole 'core' is affected by breathing. By focusing on your breath, you will become relaxed for performance, and you will also get a sense of your body's center. Just remain there focusing on your breath for about twenty seconds. [Wait for the students to complete this activity.] And, stop.

Now, using your hands go ahead and pull your body forward on the floor until you are upright on your knees. In this position you will have both hands on the floor and both knees on the floor. [Wait for the students to complete this activity.] To provide a nice stretch we are going to go into what yoga instructors call the 'cat' and the 'cow' position. While you remain on your hands and knees, arch your back and hold. Go ahead and do that. This is called 'cat.' Now go ahead and bend the center of your back down until you look as if a horse's saddle might fit nicely on your back. This is called 'cow.' As you exhale, move back to 'cat,' but when you exhale move to 'cow' (60). Please breathe at a moderate pace while you complete these activities. Please begin and alternate from 'cat' to 'cow' five times (*Actor Training*, 58–60). [Wait for the students to complete this activity.] And, stop.

From your position on your hands and knees, we are going to do a few more traditional yoga poses. These may be a little challenging, so please do what you can. Of course, you should always try to do the exercises if you possibly can. Now, from this position on your hands and knees go back to 'child's pose.' In much the same way as we got up on our hands and knees, pull your body forward using your hands; however, as you pull your body forward lift your knees off the floor, tuck your toes under and taking a few steps forward raising your midsection into what yoga instructors often call 'down dog.' I would like you to try this. Please follow me. Pull your body forward, lift your knees, tuck your toes, and push up your midsection using your ab muscles until your back looks like a pyramid. This is called 'down dog.' Hold this pose for a few seconds and breathe normally. 'Down dog' allows us to strengthen and stretch our body. [Check to see if all the students were able to complete the activity.]

Now, we are going to make the stretch a little bit more difficult and exercise the body at the same time. From 'down dog,' slowly drop your knees a bit until you are in what many of us call a 'push-up' position. Go ahead and do that. [Wait until they complete the activity.] Yoga instructors call this 'plank' position. Please bend your elbows as if you are doing a 'push-up' bringing your chest close to the floor. Yoga instructors call this pose 'chaturanga.' Go ahead and lower your 'core' to the floor and arch up like a snake. Yoga instructors call this pose 'cobra.' Next, lift your waist and go back to 'down dog.' Take some steps forward and lift your hands so you can stand. Take a few seconds to breathe, and we will repeat the sequence. [Wait about 10 seconds.] We are going to repeat the sequence. Start from 'child's pose,' to 'down dog,' then go ahead to 'plank,' which looks like the start of a 'push up,' then lower your body to 'chaturanga.' Try arching to 'cobra,' hold for a few seconds, and then go back to 'down dog.' Now lower yourself to the floor and go back to 'child's pose.' Rest for a few seconds. [Wait about five seconds.] Feel free to stand up and just walk freely through the space. [Let the students walk for a minute or two.] Go back to what we consider the audience section of the classroom and have a seat.

Today in class we focused on breathing, stretching, strengthening the body, and strengthening the core. We do this as actors to make the body more responsive on stage. This is necessary for the physical demands of some roles. I argue that strong breath support, strong body control, and a strong core allow us to be better able to pursue our 'action.' For instance, we use a *tool* to work toward achieving an *action* when something we see in our partner makes us choose that *tool*. Having a responsive not sluggish body and voice allows us to make quicker *tool* shifts. A quicker *tool* shift can be the difference between an incredibly effective response in a scene or a less than effective response. More specifically, firing off a verbal 'threat' at our scene partner that fills the theatre with a high/low pitch tone or dashing across the stage to offer quick 'physical imposition' upon our scene partner can be much more effective than softly relaying a line as a 'threat' or nonchalantly strolling over to 'physically impose' our hands on our scene partner's arms. Our voice and body must always be ready for what the scene needs in any specific moment, and we may not truly know what our scene needs in a specific moment until that very moment. Therefore, much like an athlete or a musician, we must train our instruments. As actors, our instruments are our mind, voice, and body. In what other ways are actors called upon to use the mind, voice, and body as instruments in performance? [Field student responses and hold a general discussion.] I appreciate your commentary.

Next, I will talk briefly about our following class and give you a very short assignment. In our next class we will explore presence, the physical space around our body, and ensemble work. To do these things, I want to start with an activity from Chuck Jones' book. To do that activity I need you to bring a short reading with you to class. It can be as simple as a song lyric, a poem, or a few sentences from a letter you received. It just must have some sort of special value to you. I do not necessarily want you to bear your soul to the class or share some secret song you like. I just want you to bring in something that matters to you. That means, you should not read a paragraph from a math text book (unless that paragraph is one of the most beautiful things you have ever read). Do you understand? Are there any questions? [Field student responses.] I will see you next class." [For a constructivist analysis of this lesson, instructors should see Table 7.1.]

TABLE 7.1 "Breathing, Stretching, and Strengthening"

Title:	Lesson B1 - "Breathing, Stretching, and Strengthening" Constructivist Analysis
Subject:	Acting
Level:	I
Objectives:	The students will demonstrate effective breathing, stretching, and strengthening activities for performance preparation. The students will further hypothesize the need for training the mind, voice, and body as instruments in theatrical performance.
Situation:	The students are asked to learn and practice warm-up activities that deal with stretching, strengthening, and effective breathing.
Groups:	Students will work individually during the majority of this class period on exercises for the body.
Bridge:	The students are asked to compare the physical requirements of a stage actor to the physical requirements of an athlete or musician. How are they similar? The point of this bridge is to draw a connection to something familiar. In the discussion segments of the class, the instructor can also note how certain muscles will be used during performance. This allows the student to think of himself/herself as an actor.
Exhibit:	The instructor will be moving throughout the room to check on each student's proper breathing, movement, and form. The student should do his/her best to complete the exercise as described by the instructor. If a student has health concerns that would keep him/her from safely completing the exercises, they should not do the exercise.
Reflection:	The instructor should note how well the students are working through the exercises. Some of these exercises require a high level of muscle understanding, so if students cannot do certain exercises, or are literally unfamiliar with how certain muscles work in the body, the teacher should note this. It may be necessary to take special care in completing specific exercises. This requires absolute concentration on the part of the teacher because he/she does not want students to get hurt or embarrassed for being unable to complete some exercises. If students are having difficulty during class, the instructor must make sure students do only the exercises that they can. In no way should the instructor force students to complete exercises they simply cannot do.
Assignment:	The students are supposed to bring a short reading to class with them next time. The reading should be of personal importance because it is going to be used to work on an exercise focusing on presence.

Lesson B2: "Presence, Laban kinesphere, and ensemble"

Lesson narrative

"Welcome back to class. Last class I gave you an assignment to find a reading that had special meaning to you. I assume each of you brought that with you to class today. Place that on your seat. Then, form a single file line against the wall so your shoulders are almost touching. I am going to have a seat in the center of the place we consider the audience. What I would like each of you to do is close your eyes and think about the calmest place you have ever been; we have done this before in a relaxation exercise. That place can be the beach, at a park, in the mountains for even at a beloved relative's house. Think about what that felt like. Think how warm you felt inside and how comfortable you were. While you are thinking about this place, go to the 'neutral position' we learned in a previous class where you imagined a string connected to your head. Just take a moment and remain in 'neutral,' but feel the warmth of that comfortable place.

Now think of the origin of that warmth to be your body's 'core,' the center of your body. You can picture the warmth as a glowing ball of light that resides in your 'core,' but the rays of light from that glowing ball shine out in all directions from your center. Really try to feel how that warmth offers you a sense of calmness, but also power. Take a moment to visualize that [Give the students time to visualize what I asked.] Now, allow yourself to keep that glowing ball of warmth in your 'core,' but imagine yourself leaving that peaceful place you imagined. With your eyes still closed, imagine yourself being transported from that place of comfort to our classroom right now. Go ahead and gradually open your eyes, but keep imagining that glowing ball of light in the 'core' of your body. As you open your eyes, imagine the rays of light that come from the glowing ball in your 'core' to begin to shine out in all directions filling this entire space with light. You should consider this light to be your presence. It is the light of your person that is filling the entire performance space.

The two people in the center of our line should slowly walk downstage as far as you can [Call them by name]. As you do so, still imagine that light, that presence from your 'core,' shining in all directions and filling the whole space. Go ahead and do that. As they do so, the rest of you should step either stage right or stage left to fill in the space that was left so we will have a straight line across the wall. Now, for the two of you walking downstage let that light fill the entire space. Think of your presence reaching every member of the audience who might someday be here watching you. As you approach as far as you can downstage simply stop when you get there and look into the space. Imagine your presence reaching everyone as you each turn away from each other and walk appropriately stage right or left until you come near the sides of our space. Please do that. As you approach the walls keep thinking of that light, that presence, filling the space. Then, turn around and go back to take up the right or left corner positions in the line with your classmates. Keep imagining the light. Imagine your presence filling the room even when you take your position in the line of your classmates. [Wait until they complete the requested action.] Now, the two individuals currently in the center of our line should slowly walk downstage as far as you can [Call them by name]. As you do so, still imagine that light, that presence from your 'core,' shining in all directions and filling the whole space. Let us repeat the exercise until all the students have had a chance to walk down stage center and get back in line.

Since we each have had the opportunity to walk down center, I want you to continue thinking of that light in your 'core' as your presence. This time find your own space in the room and face me. It does not matter where; it only matters that there is an arm's length between you and another person. This may mean we have to be in staggered lines filling the room. Go ahead and find a position, but keep that light shining bright from your 'core.' Do not let your presence 'go out.' [Let them find a place if they have not done so already.]

What you have experienced is the idea of stage presence. I want you to keep that idea of presence glowing brightly whenever you are or onstage. Do you understand? [Wait for the students to acknowledge 'yes' in some way.] That presence passes from your body to all the areas of our room or a theatre, but onstage other actors encounter that presence, too. There is an area about three feet around our entire body that we call our personal space. When we are not onstage, we sometimes feel awkward when others violate our personal space. For example, someone might be what we call a 'close talker.' A 'close talker' is someone who gets too close to us when he/she begins a conversation. In addition, we might feel odd when someone stands too close to us in an elevator. When we feel odd like that, we have someone violating our personal space. They are there and we can sense it. I call this personal space for ease of understanding, but movement specialist Rudolph Laban had a name for roughly the same area around us which we can reach in any direction with one arm by taking one step. He called this area our kinesphere (Newlove 17).

When we are in a play or a scene with other actors, the other actors are going to come into contact with our kinesphere; we have to get used to that. We must get used to what it feels like because we need to keep that sense of presence from our 'core' alive as we interact with other actors. We also want to be able to sense when other actors are around us, so we can react to them as necessary. Therefore, the first step in getting used to moving closely with other actors is to determine the extremes of our kinesphere. The following exercise will help each of us identify that personal space. I simply ask that you keep your sense of presence alive as we work through the next exercise together. Since each of us has already found a space to work, please go to your 'neutral position' with your arms at your sides and your feet placed firmly on the floor hip width apart and facing me. [Wait for them to do so.] During the exercise, do your best to follow. If you get confused, simply catch up when you can. Everyone will learn at a different pace. Let's begin.

While still facing me please do the following in one movement: without moving your right foot, take a large step left with your left foot while extending both arms as far left as is comfortable with your palms vertical (fingers pointing up) and face left. Now, from that position, complete the following in one movement: without moving your right foot, shift your weight back to your right foot and take a large step forward with your left foot while extending both arms as far forward as is comfortable with your palms remaining vertical (fingers pointing up) and facing me or what we will now call downstage. From that position, complete the following in one movement: without sliding your right foot, shift your weight back to your right foot and take a large step toward what we will now call upstage with your left foot while extending both arms as far upstage as is comfortable with your palms vertical (fingers pointing down this time) at waist height. Now, for the tricky part, please complete the following in one movement: raise both hands above your head as you put all your weight on your right foot and pivot your body on your right foot until you are facing what we can consider stage left and are able to take a large step left on your left foot. As you take that large step left on your left foot, extend both arms as far upstage as is comfortable with your palms vertical (fingers pointing up) and facing upstage at chest height.

From this new body position facing stage left, complete all the same movements and you will end up facing downstage. Then complete the same movements, but this time step right first and pivot on your left foot. Upon completing a clockwise circle this time, you will pivot on your right foot a fourth time and change your body position so you are facing downstage again. Finally, while facing downstage, you will then shift your weight to your left foot and take all the steps with your right foot as you turn clockwise through all those familiar bodily positions until you are once again facing downstage. This gives an actor a sense of kinesphere and it takes practice! At the completion of the exercise with a new sense of kinesphere and a new sense of presence, we can move on to some ensemble exercises.

The following exercises are Viewpoints based and allow actors to become comfortable moving and interacting with others on stage. We do these exercises after the kinesphere exercises because they are supposed to help us gain a greater sense of the personal space around us. To begin everyone should walk through the entire open space in which we have to work. Remember to move in your 'neutral positions' (arms by your sides and no hands in pockets) and keep that glowing sense of presence at the 'core' of your being. As you move, get a sense of the people around you. [Let them move through the space for a couple minutes.] Now, I would like to try something. Stop where you are and face me.

This entire exercise is based on a Viewpoints exercises from *The Viewpoints Book* by Anne Bogart and Tina Landau. Let's begin. In your mind, choose a direction in which you are going to walk and a pace at which you are going to walk. When I say walk you must walk at that constant pace in a straight line with *intention*. What I mean by intention is 'with purpose.' I do not mean run, stomp, or do some sort of strange dramatic sweep. Instead, make a decision and stick to that decision without veering. This is much the same thing as playing your *action* in a scene. When you play your *action* in a scene nothing else matters. You are simply using the text of a scene you are performing to achieve your *action*. Only the physical changes you see in your partner might make you shift tools, but you never shift *action* unless we analyzed a scene and it has several 'shifts in *action*.' Liken the movement you are about to make to playing your *action*; you are moving in a specific direction you chose to move. In your mind only decide upon the direction and pace, but do not move yet. [Wait for the actors to choose a direction and pace.] When I say go I want you to start moving in that direction; however, there are two catches to this.

The first catch is you must always move at a constant pace in your chosen direction until you come close to walls. When you get to one of those positions, you must obviously stop, and choose a different direction. Then, simply start moving again with intention in that new direction. It can be in any direction you like, but you must again walk in a straight line and at a steady pace.

The second catch is if you are going to run into another actor; do not run into another actor. Simply stop moving just before you are about to run into that person. Because this is an ensemble exercise and we are all taking care of one another, you may not start moving again until a fellow actor taps you on the shoulder (the fellow actor cannot be the one you almost ran into). When a fellow actor taps you on the shoulder, feel free to choose another direction and walk at a constant pace in that direction until you are about to run into someone else or come close to a wall. At the same time, make sure you keep that sense of presence alive in your 'core' and try to sense the kinesphere that exists around you. It is a great deal to remember, but actors have a great deal to remember when we are on stage. Do you understand all the directions? [Field any questions.] When I say go, you will begin moving. Ready, *go*. [For several minutes let the class move freely, stop near one another, tap one another on the shoulder, and change directions when required.] And, stop.

I am now going to teach you about pace. We are going to do the exact same exercise again following the exact same rules, but this time everyone must move at the same pace. I will tell you what that pace will be by saying a number from one to ten. If I say *one*, everyone will move at the same time at a very slow pace but in your chosen direction. If I say *ten*, everyone will move at the same time but in your chosen direction. The other rules of the previous exercise still apply. If you are about to bump into someone, you must stop. The only way to start moving again is to have someone tap you on the shoulder. In addition, you must change direction if you come to a wall. Are there any questions? [Field any questions.] Let's start moving at a pace of one [Let the actors move for a minute or two before choosing a different number.] And, stop. (Bogart and Landau 36–42). Thank you for your work. Go ahead and rest for a minute or two before we move on to another ensemble exercise. [Let the actors rest and get water if that is at all possible.]

It is now time to try another ensemble exercise. This entire exercise is also based on a Viewpoints exercise from *The Viewpoints Book* by Anne Bogart and Tina Landau. Again, please do your best to maintain that sense of presence emanating from your 'core' and remember the dimensions of your kinesphere around your body. We will remain standing for this exercise, so please form a medium size circle in the center of the floor. Since I will be giving directions from outside the circle, do not include me in this exercise. Please form a circle. [Wait for the students to do this, but remain outside the circle.] Face the center of the circle and make sure there is approximately one shoulder width between each person in the circle. It is important that the circle not be too small or too large because that might change the difficulty level of the exercise. In fact, a circle that is too large *or* too small increases the difficulty of the exercise. Is everyone set? [Just wait for some sort of affirmative response.]

Please start moving in a counter-clockwise direction which means to start rotating the circle to the right. Move at a modest pace and keep your focus in the center of the circle. When I clap my hands, you will all change direction at the exact same time and start moving in a clockwise direction. If you do not all move at exactly the same time, we will have to stop and start all over again. Do you understand? [Wait for some sort of affirmative response.] When I clap my hands, you will start moving in a clockwise direction. [Let the students continue moving for several seconds before clapping.] *Clap!*

When I clap my hands, you will all change direction at the exact same time and start moving in a counter-clockwise direction. If you do not all change direction at the same time, we will have to start all over again. So, listen for my clap. [Let the students continue moving for several seconds before I clap.] *Clap!*

I am going to make things a little bit more difficult. This time I am not going to clap at all. As a group, you are all going to start on your own. You will then have the option to change directions as a group or stop as a group. If you stop as a group, you will also decide the direction in which you will start moving again. Let me repeat those directions. As a group, you will all begin moving on your own in the same direction. You then have the option to stop or change direction as long as you all do it together on your own. If you do not do any of these things together as a group, I will say *stop* and you must stop and start moving again. Remember, this is an ensemble exercise, so you must keep a sense of personal presence in your 'core' while keeping in mind your kinesphere and taking care of each other as a group. You are all in this together. Do you understand? [Field any questions.] You can begin when you like (Bogart and Landau 27–28). Thank you for your efforts. Go back to your seats, and we will now look at the readings you brought to class. [Pause and wait for the students to get to their seats and find their readings.]

Let us do a test of what we have learned so far before we go into Improvisation for Movement. In Chuck Jones' book, *Make your Voice Heard: An Actor's Guide to Increased Dramatic Range through Vocal Training,* Jones shares an anecdote about famous actor John Barrymore. He heard the story from another famous actor, Anthony Quinn. Quinn states that Barrymore was about to act Shakespeare and knew his voice was not be up to the task. He sought help from voice teacher Margaret Carrington. When they met, Carrington asked Barrymore to 'pick up an apple from a bowl on her table.' She then asked Barrymore, 'Mr. Barrymore, what do you have in your hand?' Barrymore replied, 'I got a red apple.' Carrington responded, 'You have what?' Barrymore repeated, 'I got a red apple.' Carrington continued, 'I'm sorry, I don't understand.' Barrymore said. 'You don't understand? I got a red apple in my hand.' Supposedly, 'the first two or three weeks [of Barrymore's vocal training] were about making that apple sound like the juiciest, reddest apple in the world' (81).

I share this story with you because I want you to take it to heart as each of you reads what he/she brought in to class today. For several class periods we have been warming up our voices, we have worked on breathing, we have analyzed scenes, we have examined 'actions,' we have practiced repetition, and we have even examined kinesphere and stage presence. We are now going to use those things as we read our readings. That way we will know how to use those things we learned when we perform our scenes. Therefore, you are going to go to the front of the class and read your readings as if your reading is the 'juiciest, reddest apple in the world' (81). I am joking, of course, you do not have an apple, but you do have a personal reading you would like to share I find it easier to explore what we learned by applying it to something we feel strongly about before we start using everything we learned on our scenes. To make this easier and work with our system, I am even going to give you an *action*. You will be playing 'to get someone to see things my way' as you each read your readings. Can you think of a time when you had something important you wanted another person to understand like you did? That is your *as if*. Take a few moments and think of an *as if*. When have you tried 'to get someone to see things your way'? [Give them a few moments to think of a specific moment.] Trying to use everything we have learned, we are going to read our readings individually on stage in front of the rest of the class. Remember the presence and movement exercises and keep in mind your action. Allow that glowing light to fill the room. Do you have an *as if* for the *action* 'to get someone to see things my way'? [Wait for affirmative responses.] Do you understand what I am asking you to do? [Field student responses.] Good. Who would like to go first? [Let the volunteer go first or chose someone to go first if there are no volunteers. Then have each student complete his/her reading.].

Today we worked on presence, kinesphere, ensemble work, and individual readings. Everything we worked on today is applicable to your scene work and all the work you will ever do on stage. It is important to understand that. It is also important to understand that an actor must juggle many things at the same time during a performance. As we move forward in our class, I hope you keep this in mind. In our next class we will look even more closely at movement. I look forward to working with you again; thank you for your work today. I will see you next time." [For a constructivist analysis of this lesson, instructors should see Table 7.2.]

TABLE 7.2 "Presence, Laban Kinesphere, and Ensemble"

Title:	Lesson B2 - "Presence, Laban Kinesphere, and Ensemble" Constructivist Analysis
Subject:	Acting
Level:	I
Objectives:	The students will adapt their "neutral position" to express presence. The students practice connecting with their "cores." The students will integrate movement with presence, intention, and "action." The students will integrate movement with presence, intention, and "action" at various paces. The students will experiment with kinesphere and ensemble interaction. The students will collaborate. Each student will complete a personal performance (a reading) that will ask them to formally construct a solid performance using presence and an "action."
Situation:	The students will perform a series of exercises to understand presence, kinesphere, and working with an ensemble. These exercises can be used in future classes as a "warm-up" and/or knowledge refreshers.
Groups:	The students will work together as a large ensemble, but they will also perform individually. If the instructor chooses, or if time remains, students will also work in dyads using "repetition."
Bridge:	The students are connecting past knowledge to new knowledge about presence, kinesphere, and ensemble work. They will be asked to modify their personal "neutral position" to accommodate presence. They will also use the already learned concept of "action" and "as if" in conjunction with presence in a short performance.
Exhibit:	The students will modify the "neutral" position to accommodate presence. The students will also practice moving with presence both individually and in groups. The instructor should not expect perfection, but he/she should require participation.
Reflection:	Feedback should be given orally to individuals during class to help students grasp the concepts being taught. Feedback on paper can be given to students, but I find that a bit overwhelming. I prefer offering "positive comments" and a single "constructive criticism" verbally to every student after his/her reading. Of course, participation grades would be appropriate. The instructor must also note how he/she functioned in this lesson. Often times, directions must be modified for understanding.
Assignment:	The students are to continue learning their lines, practice their breathing exercises, and journal (if assigned to do so).

Lesson B3: "Improvisation for movement"
Lesson narrative

At this point in the semester, I suggest warming up with a combination of body and voice exercises learned over the course of the semester. I always end with one or two quick rounds of repetition, as well. It is impossible to do all the warm-up activities the students have learned. Therefore, as a Constructivist, I use what seemed most helpful to a particular group of students. If a class looks particularly sluggish on a certain day, I use activities that made them smile or chuckle in the past.

"It is nice to see everyone again. We have not worked extensively on movement within a performance, so today we are going to do just that. we are going to 'begin to learn how best to balance and share the stage, how good movement and blocking tell the story as well as dialogue, and how best to put the audience's focus wherever it may belong' (Urcioli 115). You may have seen improvisation on television. Who can tell me the purpose of improvisation? [Field student responses.] While everything you said can happen in improvisation, I want you to think of improvisation a bit differently in this class. I would like to use improvisation to practice moving on stage during a performance. It is true we have done several movement exercises, but we have not worked with movement specifically tied to an actual performance. That is what we want to focus on today. In an improvisation, I can let you all play with moving around on stage while I offer a little help from off stage. I find that if I start talking about movement and blocking in improvisation, students take some of those ideas and create their own movement ideas when performing a scene. This does not mean that I will refrain from giving you movement tips during your scene rehearsals; I will if you need it. We just have to see. When I eventually notice you are freely moving on your own in support of your action, and only in support of your action, I will let you take over moving on instinct. Moving on instinct, in support of your action alone, can be very difficult. Therefore, think of my movement suggestions as you do the *as if* game: the suggestions are like training wheels on a bicycle. When you do not need them anymore, we can take them away.

Let us begin with a game called 'Dubbing.' I first learned about this exercise from my improvisation teacher in New York, Paul Urcioli ("Discovering Ensemble" 113). In this exercise we are going to have two people seated and two people moving. One of the seated participants will sit right center in a chair and another will sit left center in a chair. They will be offering the dialogue for the scene we are going to view. Standing center will be two other participants. They will be acting out the scene by providing the movement. As you may have guessed, the participant seated right center will provide the voice for the actor stage right and the participant seated left center will provide the voice for the actor stage left. The idea is that the individuals who are seated only have to worry about dialogue, and those standing only have to worry about movement. You do not have to do more than one thing at a time.

I will begin by providing the seated participants with a 'who, what, where, when, and why.' I may give you an innocuous scene such as two siblings playing catch after school. On the other hand, I may give you something very specific, or even difficult, like a lousy magician and a TV weatherperson waiting for their food order at a fast food restaurant in Atlanta's airport before catching a morning flight to Vermont. The job of the seated participants is to provide dialogue, while the standing participants move accordingly. In this exercise, those who will be moving must keep in mind standard stage conventions such as not normally turning your back to the audience, but they must fulfill the movements required by the dialogue. Those who will be providing dialogue must provide dialogue that can lead to possible stage movement. In other words, you should not say something like 'let's jump off this mountain.' You must work to support each other. The goal is to make sure the scene makes sense, while allowing the individuals who are moving to practice stage movement. Again, the idea is not to be funny or hurtful. It is also not to stump your partner, and you cannot negate anything by saying 'no.' Do I have any volunteers willing to provide dialogue? [Ask the volunteers to come up and have a seat, or choose participants.] Do I have any volunteers willing to try movement? [Ask those volunteers to come up, or choose participants.]

Before we begin, I want to be clear about what I am looking for in this exercise. In a normal performance we can use both language and movement to tell a story. This exercise splits the two. Those actors who are speaking must focus on language to tell the story, while those actors who are moving must focus on movement to tell the story. Therefore, a successful performance will be generated if everyone on stage works together in his/her given mediums to produce a coherent piece. This activity also forces individual actors to focus on the importance of just language or just movement on stage. That is something we all must learn to be successful performers. Are there any questions? [Field questions.] If there are no more questions, please take your places and we will begin. Ready. Go. [Let the performance continue for three to five minutes or until the actors seem unable to proceed.] And, stop. I appreciate your work. I would like the audience to tell us what was successful in this performance and what might need improvement. Take into consideration how each performer handled his/her given performance medium. [Field responses while stressing the importance of both language and action in the theatre.]

The second exercise we are going to do today is called 'Japanese Rock Garden': 'a nonverbal exercise where a group of actors go into the designated playing space and form a series of tableaux' (Urcioli 114). The audience will 'close their eyes between the pictures to maximize the effect of seeing only the tableaux [,] leaving the transitions the business of the players only' (114). The individuals who provided dialogue in the last exercise should come up and stand in front of the audience. [Let those volunteers come forward, or choose their actors.] Those in the audience, close your eyes while the five actors on stage are going to move and form a tableau. Audience, please close your eyes and actors move into a position. [Give them time to move around before calling 'stop.'] Audience, please open your eyes. What do you see? [Field audience responses.] Let's try that again. Audience, please close your eyes and actors move into a position. [Give them time to move around before calling 'stop.'] Audience, please open your eyes. What do you see? [Field audience responses. The students may have to be encouraged to use their imaginations to see the stage pictures that have been formed.] Those actors should take a seat and different actors who have not yet done movement today should to come up. We are going to repeat what this first group did, but it is your job to choose a different tableaux. [Thank you.] Everyone can have a seat. What have you learned about stage pictures created by groups of people in this exercise? [Field student responses. It is essential for them to realize that simple positioning of the body or bodies produces meaning for members of the audience. The students may not be consciously aware of this. Therefore, this activity helps them see why movement and positioning on stage is so important. In addition, they learn that an actor is truly in control of *meaning making* at all times when on stage. Meaning is created by more than just language and movement.]

For our final activity we are going to do today, we are going to use elements from both of these previous exercises. The activity we are going to do is called 'Two Minute Movie.' I certainly want you to enjoy the activity, but it serves a greater purpose than providing a good time or allowing you to be silly. At its base level, this activity requires you to develop aural and visual 'signposts' that allow the audience to understand the story of the film. This means you will have to quickly choose what is most important to say and what is most important for the audience to see. If I reduce your time allotment to one minute, you will have to determine which 'signposts' need to be skipped, combined, or edited for time while also making sure the audience can follow your abbreviated version. If I ask you to do the performance in less than a minute, you will have to make further edits. This can be very difficult, but also very rewarding. The reward of the exercise is that you will get an impression of what is absolutely necessary for successful storytelling. This is a valuable lesson to learn in the theatre, because it is fundamental to impressive acting. Actors who are able to tell a story while also using all the skills they learned in training and rehearsal just to act are laudable.

Therefore, I am going to give each person a number between one and five. [Count them all out by simply counting one through five down a row or at random.] We will use theatre terms to indicate where groups should meet. Everyone who was given the number one should come up and meet stage left, those who were given number two should meet upstage center, those who were given number three should meet stage right, those who were given number four should meet stage center, and those who were given number five should meet downstage center. Go ahead and take those positions.

I have grouped you according to number because those given the same number will be working together. Therefore, everyone who received number one will work together, those who received number two will work together, etc. Right now each group should decide and work with a movie you all have seen. You should be quite familiar with the movie or be able to refresh the memories of those who are unfamiliar with it rather quickly because you are going to act out the entire movie in two minutes. Go ahead and pick a film together. I will walk around and check on your progress. [Give the groups a few minutes to decide upon a movie.] Now that you have come up with a movie, I am going to give you around five or six minutes to talk over how you are going to improvise the movie. Remember, you must perform the entire movie in two minutes, so you have to be precise with your dialogue and stage pictures. That is why we practiced with both elements just moments ago. Go ahead and talk over your improvisation with your group. [Give the groups five minutes to talk over the improvisation.] Now everyone should have a seat except for group one. Group one has the stage.

Group one I am going to give you two minutes to act out your entire film. Please tell the audience what film you chose. [Wait for them to tell the audience.] When I say go, you will have two minutes to act out the whole movie. I will give you a verbal warning at the one minute mark, the thirty second mark, the fifteen second mark, and I will say stop. Get ready, and *go*. [Time the group as stated.] And, *stop*. Audience, what did you think? [Ask the audience to give positive comments and constructive criticism to group one.] Thank you group one, but I want to test your storytelling abilities a bit more. Please present your film again. This time you have to do it in one minute. I must stress it is crucial that this activity not fall into absurdity or nonsense. You must keep the integrity of the story by focusing on the visual and aural signposts. Being able to tell a story with purposefully chosen words, movements, and tableaux is what you must take away from this exercise, not how to be funny or absurd. Nevertheless, do not misunderstand me. The exercise can be humorous, but the humor should not come from sheer chaos. [Ask them to do the entire movie once again in 30 seconds and finally, one last time, in 15 seconds. Again, I stress the importance of accurate, albeit condensed, storytelling.] Thank you group one. What did the rest of you think of group one's performance? [Field student responses and ask them specifically about the accuracy of the storytelling.] It is group two's turn to show us their work, etc. [Cycle through each group]. Alright everyone, please have a seat in what we have determined to be the audience section of the room.

Thank you for your work. Today we worked quite a bit with both improvised dialogue and movement. This class was important because in your scenes you will also be improvising. You will not be using improvised dialogue, of course, but you will be improvising how you deliver the dialogue and the movements you choose. Your movements will be motivated by actively trying to achieve your *action*. While you are trying to achieve your *action*, you also must take into consideration things like not turning your back to the audience for no reason. It is a great deal to remember, and that is why we have rehearsal both during class and outside of class. It is very important to remember that rehearsal is essential to a solid performance. In the next several days we will be repeating many of the exercises we have covered so far, you will have time to work with your partner on your scenes, and I will expect you to do some rehearsal outside of class. I do not expect you to rehearse every day, but at least call each other up on the phone and run lines about three times per week. Is that understood? [Wait for some sort of acknowledgement.] Acting is not easy; it is important to remember that. For your homework, phone one another and run lines so you have your lines fully memorized. Remember, we are in this together. I will see you next class." [For a constructivist analysis of this lesson, instructors should see Table 7.3.]

TABLE 7.3 "Improvisation for Movement"

Title:	Lesson B3 - "Improvisation for Movement" Constructivist Analysis
Subject:	Acting
Level:	I
Objectives:	The students will learn improvisation in order to become familiar with stage movement.
Situation:	The students will partake in three improvisation activities to become familiar with stage movement.
Groups:	The students will be in groups of four or five for today's exercises.
Bridge:	Today's class uses many of the terms we have used in class already. This provides a cognitive link between all the exercises. The students will also be able to answer questions such as, "What is improvisation?" Questions like these will help the students develop a schema that has to do with acting (or schemata that work together). The instructor can also create a verbal bridge for the students by side coaching the improvisations.
Exhibit:	The instructor will view all students in improvisations. Both positive comments and constructive criticism will be provided. The teacher must keep track of who performed what activity so every student gets a chance to do an improvisation.
Reflection:	Feedback should be given orally to individuals during class to help students grasp the concepts being taught. The instructor must also note how he/she functioned in this lesson. Often times, directions must be modified for student understanding.
Assignment:	The students are to call their scene partners on the telephone and run lines. All scenes should be memorized for next class.

Works cited

Adrian, Barbara. *Actor Training the Laban Way: An Integrated Approach to Voice, Speech, and Movement*. New York: Allworth Press, 2008. Print.

Adrian, Barbara. "An Introduction to Laban Movement Analysis for Actors: A Historical, Theoretical, and Practical Perspective." *Movement for Actors*. Ed. Nicole Potter. New York: Allworth Communications, 2002. Print.

Barry, Cecily. "That Secret Voice." *The Vocal Vision: Views on Voice by 24 Leading Teachers, Coaches & Directors*. Eds. Marion Hampton and Barbara Acker. New York: Applause, 1998. Print

Bogart, Anne and Tina Landau. *The Viewpoints Book: A Practical Guide to Viewpoints and Composition*. New York: Theatre Communications Group, 2005. Print.

Jones, Chuck. *Make Your Voice Heard: An Actor's Guide to Increased Dramatic Range through Vocal Training*. New York: Back Stage Books, 2005. Print.

Newlove, Jean and John Dalby. *Laban for All*. London: Nick Hern, 2004. Print.

Urcioli, Paul. "Discovering Ensemble and Impulse through Improvisation." *Movement for Actors*. Ed. Nicole Potter. New York: Allworth Press, 2002. Print.

8
CLOSURE

This book presents a constructivist approach to teaching acting at the college and secondary levels. This constructivist approach to teaching voice/diction and movement, in conjunction with David Mamet's Practical Aesthetics, can provide a thorough set of lessons focused on developing the performance skills of the beginning actor. There is a call for this constructivist approach because, as Maxine Green states in her article "On Teaching and Learning in the Arts":

> In the realm of the arts, as in other realms of meaning, learning goes on more fruitfully in atmospheres of interchange and shared discoveries. There must be those who can point out what is not yet noticed, not yet heard, people who can provoke the young to reach beyond where they are. To reach beyond is to realize that there exist a tradition and a community of knowers, of seekers none of whom has the final answer to any question, all of whom are engaged in a communal construction of knowledge. It is as much social as it is individual, as much part of a culture as it is personally, privately constructed. (116)

This idea applies to the acting classroom where individuals, dyads, groups, and entire classrooms work toward developing the skills necessary to make theatre art come alive. Granted, this is not an easy task; however, I found it almost impossible when I was trying to teach acting according to the traditional methods of education I learned in my teacher education program.

In his famous book, *Pedagogy of the Oppressed*, Paulo Freire refers to this traditional method of education as the "banking model" of education. It juxtaposes Maxine Greene's vision of constructivist education because in the banking model of education,

> The students are not called upon to know, but to memorize the contents narrated by the teacher. Nor do the students practice any act of cognition, since the object towards which that act should be directed is the property of the teacher rather than a medium evoking the critical reflection of both teacher and students. Hence in the name of the 'preservation of culture and knowledge' we have a system which achieves neither true knowledge nor true culture. (Freire 68)

Theatre instructors have been challenging this model for several years because of the nature of our subject. We employ various activities and exercises that do not resemble things like memorizing multiplication tables and taking a test over them, but I still felt my college and secondary students needed something more. I was not simply asking students to do things like memorize lines, stand on stage, and recite lines exactly as I told them; however, asking them to simply follow my blocking was pretty close to memorizing multiplication tables. I found constructivism and Practical Aesthetics because I was searching for a better way to serve my students. I wanted my students to function as actors, not as marionettes.

Constructivism is also valuable because it does more than work against the banking model of education; it creates a different type of learning. According to Gabler and Schroeder in *Constructivist Methods for the Secondary Classroom: Engaged Minds*:

> Two arenas need to be integrated to shift students from the familiar role of listener to that of active learner: affect and constructivist methods. By *affect* we mean state of mind and state of being, the student's belief in self-empowerment. By *constructivist methods* we mean instructional templates for lessons and units that encourage students to be critical thinkers and independent learners, with the teacher acting as a mentor and facilitator. (xvii)

By its very basic nature, constructivism assumes that the power to learn is in the hands of the students. This promotes self-efficacy. Essentially, students' current knowledge and past experiences are taken into consideration and valued, students are continually asked to process what they are learning, students act cooperatively with one another and the instructor during lessons, student opinions are discussed, and the instructor treats each student as a fellow human being engaged in the pursuit of knowledge. This personal acknowledgement of the student as an active member of a class is why he/she feels invested in the classroom. When coupled with constructivist instructional templates like those created by Gagnon and Collay in *Designing for Learning: Six Elements in Constructivist Classrooms*, which I have used as a template for every lesson in this book, students may also become critical thinkers and independent learners. Certainly, the instructor must do his/her best to function as mentor and facilitator; however, student investment plus lessons specifically tailored to foster critical thinking and independent learning should be the goal of any instructor. For me, Practical Aesthetics paved the way toward that goal. This is better explained by another simile.

Practical Aesthetics allowed me to start thinking about acting as an iceberg that I must help students *see in its totality* rather than as a storehouse of information to be deposited into currently spacious minds. I cannot take credit for creating the iceberg metaphor, but it aptly describes what I think all education should truly be like. Simply put, there is more to true teaching and true education than we often think.

For example, in his book *Meisner for Teens: A Life of True Acting*, Larry Silverberg calls upon the iceberg analogy to explain that "acting is not about the words" (56). That was my problem early in my career. I was looking only at the words, and the students were only looking at the words. Unfortunately, those words on paper or on the computer screen did not reveal everything we needed to know; words on paper are not enough to teach a student how to act. In fact, Silverberg developed the analogy from a quote by Peter Brook, author of *The Empty Space*. Brook states:

> A word does not start as a word—it is an end product which begins as an impulse, stimulated by attitude and behavior which dictate the need for expression. This process occurs inside the dramatist; it is repeated inside the actor. Both may only be conscious of the words, but both for the author and then for the actor the word is a small visible portion of a gigantic unseen formation. Some writers attempt to nail down their meaning and intentions in stage directions and explanations, yet we cannot help being struck by the fact that the best dramatists explain themselves the least. They recognize that the only way to find the true path to the speaking of a word is through a process that parallels the original creative one. This can neither be by passed nor simplified (15).

If "for the actor the word is a small visible portion of a gigantic unseen formation," I was searching for a way to teach students how to discover Silverberg's entire acting iceberg (56–57). I believe one way to uncover the acting iceberg, in a teachable way, is to use constructivist pedagogy to teach Practical Aesthetics, voice/diction, and movement.

For example, I can tell students they should focus on the other actor in a scene, but that does not mean they do it. Only through repetition exercises did my students start to realize why they had to focus on the other person rather than themselves. By focusing on another, the scene becomes alive and as Meisner would say "in the moment." Unfortunately, Meisner never wrote an acting text; I would have enjoyed reading it. He tried to write one, but he gave up because he thought it was "foolish, even wrong, to attempt to write one" (*Sanford Meisner on Acting* xvii). Nevertheless, I looked elsewhere and found exactly what I needed. I was finally able to construct a series of lessons useful for the acting instructor by combining Practical Aesthetics and constructivism with exercises in voice/diction and movement.

My series of lessons was created with the intent to construct individual, detailed, integrated, and swiftly accessible schematic maps that offer to a student how to perform as a theatre actor at any given time. I use repetition and its hopefully successful creation of "focus on the other actor" as a constant through-line. With this in mind, from being rehearsed in each lesson and constantly referenced by the instructor, students are guided through constructivist acting exercises that continue to build upon each other. For instance, the "as if game" builds upon repetition because the game requires the actor to interact with his/her partner in virtually the same fashion. The difference is that partners must talk out their "as ifs" as they pursue their action; however, "tool" choices are still based on what they see in their partners during the various moments of interaction. Likewise, the actors are to do the same type of "tool" shifting after they memorize their lines. This means that even the actual performance of a scene on stage is quite similar to repetition, which is the very first exercise learned and constantly rehearsed in the classroom.

Similarly, the voice/diction and movement exercises are closely tied to the "as if game" and the scene performance itself. During these exercises the instructor continually reminds students that any voice and/or movement choices are made in service of the "action." They are not done at random; they serve no other purpose except to serve the actor as he/she pursues his/her "action" in the "as if game" and even on stage during formal performance.

This integration and tightly bound process of learning how to act is unlike the processes taught in many familiar texts. The processes do serve an actor in performance, but they do not always share a *schematic link*. Instead, it is believed that the actor who participates in various games and exercises will automatically transfer the material from the classroom to the stage. Using constructivist pedagogy to teach Practical Aesthetics provides transfer because each new acting exercise is built upon the previous exercise. Each exercise is inextricably linked. This link also exists between the exercises and what happens on stage during a performance. In essence, what happens in the rehearsal hall also happens on stage.

A second reason Practical Aesthetics has served me well is because students learn a limited, distinct, and useful vocabulary. Students are then able to discuss performances with one another and the instructor in intelligent ways using that vocabulary. Deep discussions are also facilitated by this vocabulary because students become part of a "language community."

A third reason Practical Aesthetics has served me well in a constructivist acting class is because of its limited breadth and great depth. College and secondary level students have a greater repertoire of learning sources, but still need this material's depth. Secondary students, however, are able to master a limited number of exercises defined by the education system itself. Secondary students often receive minimum breadth and minimum depth because the theatre arts classroom usually only has one text.

For example, *Theatre: Art in Action*, *The Stage and the School*, and *Basic Drama Projects* are each meant to be used for four years. Therefore, they must attempt to cover as much about theatre as possible in a limited number of pages. The rest is up to the instructor. I may be generalizing, but I doubt any theatre instructor would argue that any of these texts contains enough material to teach secondary students everything there is to know about theatre. Theatre instructors often end up supplementing their classes with what they learned in college. This lack of support in the form of multiple texts and teaching tools is in sharp contrast to what is available to many other departments. Secondary school mathematics departments, for instance, have books and supplemental instructor support materials for algebra, geometry, trigonometry, calculus, etc. In addition, mathematics departments usually utilize multiple levels of texts within each branch of mathematics. Therefore, different performance levels in algebra, geometry, and calculus require different texts and different sets of instructor support materials. We do not have many of these resources in theatre at the secondary level—which is why this book will be part of my Theatre Education courses which train future secondary theatre instructors AND my college acting classes. It is up to the instructor to make up for the lack of materials. I am not saying texts make or break education. I am saying that theatre instructors, whether college or secondary level, should have access to the same sorts of immediately available support materials that others do. That is why I wrote this book. It is applicable to the college instructor and secondary instructor because of its depth.

On the other hand, college texts like Cohen's *Acting One*, Benedetti's *The Actor at Work*, and Hagen's *Respect for Acting* contain great breadth but face the opposite problem. They are difficult to digest completely in a semester or two. For example, I was once asked to teach Acting I at a college that required me to use Stanley Kahan's *Introduction to Acting* (3rd ed.). If one includes the glossary, the text has 367 pages. It was virtually impossible to even scratch the surface of the text while trying to teach young beginning actors how to perform. As an instructor, I would much rather tackle the limited breadth and great depth of Practical Aesthetics using a constructivist approach to teaching acting. The often overwhelming breadth of some acting texts and the underwhelming breadth of secondary texts have not served me or my students well in the past. Therefore, I manifest, via individually created meticulous lesson plans followed by constructivist lesson blueprints, my approach to teaching beginning actors.

Now the field is ripe for further research dealing with Practical Aesthetics, constructivism, and curriculum content in the theatre classroom. In *Signs of Change: New Directions in Theatre Education*, Joan Lazarus calls for the use of constructivism in the theatre classroom because it is one of her "Principles of Best Practice Learning" (34). Because Practical Aesthetics lends itself to constructivist methodologies I believe it can qualify as a best practice; however, that thesis needs further verification. In addition, possible areas of research in Practical Aesthetics include an examination of who might currently be teaching it at the secondary and/or the college level; the role of the director within the system; qualitative studies on schools using Practical Aesthetics; gender in a system that can often foster competition; what texts, if any, are being used; and student reactions to the system. Since it is a professional training system, other areas of interest might be case studies of universities and schools that train actors using a professional system, the qualifications of those teaching acting, and the role of a professionally modeled theatre program at a college or secondary school.

In addition, it is not out of the realm of possibility to suggest the use of Practical Aesthetics outside the university or school. Any type of sales position as well as the fields of law, business, politics, public speaking, and even non-profit work could benefit from the succinct way Practical Aesthetics trains an individual to convince others. Research could be conducted to study the system's applicability and usability in these areas. This could also lead to interdisciplinary work within educational institutions and cooperation with corporate agencies.

Areas of research that deal with constructivism itself might also be considered. These include qualitative studies on constructivist pedagogy in theatre at the college and secondary level, a study that examines outcomes from using constructivist pedagogy versus a traditional approach in the theatre classroom, and work that examines student reactions to constructivism in theatre classes. Other related studies that come to mind might deal with what theatre instructors are actually teaching in the acting classroom right now, scholarship that questions the reliance on or avoidance of theatre textbooks in colleges or schools, and qualitative studies on what students actually want to learn in their theatre classes. In fact, what students want to learn in their theatre classes brings me back to why acting instructors might consider the approach I have outlined in this book.

Essentially, the world has changed since George Pierce Baker's first drama courses at Harvard and his teaching career at Yale. Over the past 15 years, I have noticed that students enrolling in theatre classes want and need different things. They want to learn public speaking skills, they want to work cooperatively in groups, they want to gain confidence, they wish to be on the television show *Glee*, and/or they sincerely hope to someday make a film or Broadway debut. The sheer popularity of the 2013 *Sound of Music Live*, viewed by "18.470 million viewers," and the plethora of Broadway Jr. Musicals tell me students are interested in formal performance (Kondolojy). This has already been noted by academics in the popular press. According to Lynn O'Shaughnessy, a former college admissions dean, "If your child wants to major in musical theater or some other performing art, go ahead and blame it on *Glee, American Idol* or *America's Got Talent*" (*U.S. News & World Report*). In fact, my former acting students at Arizona State University, who are not theatre majors, made the following comments to me in writing: "I want to specifically know what separates a good performance from a bad one," "I feel as though I wasn't given the right tools for acting in high school ... I'm relieved to know that I can be starting over fresh," and "I have had a quickly growing interest in acting for film or TV ... My good bioengineer friend and I spent a chunk of the past year and a half brainstorming a video game series ... we quickly determined it would be a much better TV show. It would be awesome to see something come of that within the next ten years or so."

Other students made it a point to address the Practical Aesthetics system: "I personally do like using the 'as ifs' coming into the scene since for me it makes acting out the scene way easier," "The 'as if' is more important than the lines itself, because without the 'as if' my lines are going to be bland," and "The concepts I've learned like practical aesthetics and actions ... are very simple but make a lot of sense. It is a sweet and simple way to act ... I am really interested by this technique. I'm surprised it isn't more widespread and taught more. I definitely have a better grasp on how to perform on stage."

Finally, others commented on how my class affected their lives: "One of the most important things that I gained from this class was confidence. I became more confident with myself and I'm not afraid to take risks and just go with it," "This class is definitely the most memorable class that I have taken at ASU since I am a business major and it is so different ... I learned it is easy to alter someone's perception of you just by using some of the simple methods that you've taught us," and "It is safe to say that I've never been so aware that a course was actively changing the way I think, speak and act in every real-life situation. The way I approach conversations, personal interacting, even my essay writing is evolving so rapidly it's making my head spin. Ever realize that there is not a waking moment of our life we are not communicating?"

We need to be able to take students further—*where they want to go* as well as *where they need to go*. For me, this meant turning to Practical Aesthetics and constructivism. The plan of instruction I have outlined in this book can help college students learn how to be performers via visible steps of instruction. In addition, Practical Aesthetics and constructivism still allow a secondary instructor to fulfill the taxonomic requirements of the inevitable core curriculum that all schools may soon adopt.

My contribution to the field of theatre studies shows future theatre teachers and colleagues one way to teach acting. By sharing a theatrical vocabulary between instructor and student, working toward depth rather than breadth, fostering student empowerment, developing critical thinking, and providing independent and cooperative learning activities in a safe environment where students can "guess and be wrong," instructors can use Practical Aesthetics and constructivism to help students develop an acting schema. The possibility of developing an advanced acting schema can give students pride in their work, provide a sense of achievement, and continue to bring joy to performers and audience members in a society dominated by enticing algorithmic technology.

Works cited

Benedetti, Robert. *The Actor at Work*. 6th ed. Boston: Pearson, 2009. Print.
Brook, Peter. *The Empty Space*. New York: Atheneum, 1968. Print.
Cohen, Robert. *Acting One*. 5th ed. New York: McGraw-Hill, 2008. Print.

Freire, Paulo. *Pedagogy of the Oppressed*. Translated by Myra Bergman Ramos. New York: The Seabury Press, 1970. Print.

Gabler, Ina Claire and Michael Schroeder. *Constructivist Methods for the Secondary Classroom: Engaged Minds*. Boston: Pearson Education, 2003. Print.

Greene, Maxine. "On Teaching and Learning in the Arts." *Constructivism: Theory, Perspectives, and Practice*. Ed. Catherine T. Fosnot. New York: Teachers College Press, 2005. Print.

Hagen, Uta and Haskel Frankel. *Respect for Acting*. New York: Macmillan, 1973. Print.

Kahan, Stanley. *Introduction to Acting*. 3rd ed. Boston: Allyn and Bacon, 1991. Print.

Kondolojy, Amanda. "'The Sound of Music Live!' Gives NBC its Best Thursday in Total Viewers Since 2004, Excluding Sports." zap2it.com. TV by the Numbers. December 6, 2013. Web. February 21, 2013. http://tvbythenumbers.zap2it.com /2013/12/06/the-sound-of-music-live-gives-nbc-its-best-thursday-in-total-viewers-since-2004-excluding-sports/220600/.

Lazarus, Joan. *Signs of Change: New Directions in Theatre Education*. Rev. and amplified ed. Bristol: Intellect, 2012. Print.

Meisner, Sanford and Dennis Longwell. *Sanford Meisner on Acting*. New York: Vintage Books, 1990, Print.

O'Shaughnessy, Lynn. "Six College Admission Tips for Artistic Students." *U.S. News & World Report*. November 9, 2010. Web. February 12, 2014. www.usnews. com/education/ blogs/ the-college-solution/2010/11/09/6-college-admissions-tips-for-artistic-students.

Schanker, Harry H, and Katharine A. Ommanney. *The Stage and the School*. 9th ed. New York: McGraw-Hill Educational, 2005. Print.

Silverberg, Larry. *Meisner for Teens: A Life of True Acting*. Hanover, N.H: Smith and Kraus, 2010. Print.

Tanner, Fran A. *Basic Drama Projects*. 8th ed. Logan, Iowa: Perfection Learning, 2009. Print.

Taylor, Robert D., Robert D. Strickland and Lisa Abel. *Theatre: Art in Action*. Lincolnwood, IL: National Textbook Co., 1999. Print.

APPENDIX

Teaching materials

Acting Introduction – Suggested Course Calendar

(lessons may also be taught in order by number or in an order that suits classroom needs)During Week 1: Lesson M1 and Lesson M2

During Week 2: Lesson M3
Choose Scene Partners

During Week 3: Lesson M4
Three Copies of Scene #1 Due (one copy should be given to the instructor)

During Week 4: Lesson M5 and Lesson M6
Scene Analysis #1 Due

During Week 5: Lesson V/B1 and Lesson V/B2

During Week 6: Lesson V/B3 and Lesson M7

During Week 7: Lesson V/B4 and Lesson M8
Journal Check #1 - Seven One Page Typed Weekly Journal Entries Due

During Week 8: Lesson V/B5 and Lesson M9
Choose Scene #2 Partners (this scene will function as the final exam)

During Week 9: Lesson V/B6
Three Copies of Scene #2 Due (one copy should be given to the instructor)

During Week 10: **PERFORM SCENE #1** (effort trumps perfection in this performance)

During Week 11: Repeat Select Lessons M6–M9 and V/B1–V/B6 for Mastery
Scene Analysis #2 Due

During Week 12: Repeat Select Lessons M6–M9 and V/B1–V/B6 for Mastery
During Week 13: Repeat Select Lessons M6–M9 and V/B1–V/B6 for Mastery
During Week 14: Repeat Select Lessons M6–M9 and V/B1–V/B6 for Mastery
During Week 15: Repeat Select Lessons M6–M9 and V/B1–V/B6 for Mastery
Journal Check #2 - Eight One Page Typed Journal Entries Due

Final Exam: **PERFORM SCENE #2**

Constructivist Lesson Analysis Blueprint

Title:

Subject:
Level:

Objectives: [anticipated educational outcomes]

Situation: [a specific goal students must reach by working together]

Groups: [configuration of students during the lesson and materials they may use]

Bridge: [concept/story that illustrates how prior knowledge and new knowledge will be linked]

Exhibit: [public or interpersonal presentation of what has been learned]

Reflection: [students and instructor process what has taken place in the lesson]

A. Constructivist teachers use raw data and primary sources, along with manipulative, interactive and physical materials.
C. When framing tasks, constructivist teachers use cognitive terminology such as "classify," "analyze," "predict," and "create."
D. Constructivist teachers allow student responses to drive lessons, shift instructional strategies, and alter content.
E. Constructivist teachers inquire about students' understanding of those concepts.
F. Constructivist teachers encourage students to engage in dialogue, both with the teacher and with one another.
G. Constructivist teachers encourage student inquiry by asking thoughtful, open-ended questions and encouraging students to ask questions of each other.
H. Constructivist teachers seek elaboration of students' initial responses.
I. Constructivist teachers engage students in experiences that might engender contradictions to their initial hypotheses and then encourage discussion.
J. Constructivist teachers allow wait time after posing questions.
K. Constructivist teachers provide time for students to construct relationships and create metaphors.
L. Constructivist teachers nurture students' natural curiosity through frequent use of the learning cycle model.

This lesson plan format was modified from Gagon and Collay (2006). "Objectives" and bracketed text have been added by the author.

Constructivist Lesson Planning Sheet

Title:	
Subject: Level:	
Objectives:	
Situation:	
Groups:	
Bridge:	
Exhibit:	
Reflection:	

Name_____

Repetition: The Core Exercise in Practical Aesthetics

<u>Repetition Level I:</u> What do you literally see "about" your partner?
[Examples: (1) You see your partner smiling, so you say to your partner: "You are smiling."]

Repetition Level II: What might that which you see mean?
[Example: (1) You see your partner smiling. (2) The smile must mean something, so you say to your partner: "You are happy."]

<u>Repetition Level III:</u> What might that which you see actually infer at a deeper level?
[Example: (1) You see your partner smiling. (2) The smile must mean something. (3) You infer that the smile means something deeper than just generic happiness, so you say to your partner: "You think you are really good at this exercise!"]

Name_____

Analyzing the Scene: Student Worksheet

Name of the Play_____
Scene_____
Your Character_____
The Other Character in the Scene_____
(1) What is the character <u>literally doing</u>?

(2) What does the character <u>want</u>?

(3) What is the character's "<u>action</u>?"

(4) When did I play that same action in my personal life?
It is "<u>as if</u>" I _____to _____
when _____.

(5) What might your "<u>cap</u>" look like in this scene? A "<u>cap</u>"
is the physical gesture *your scene partner might make*
when you achieve your "action."

Some Examples of "Actions" Handout

"An action must:

1. be physically capable of being done.
2. be fun to do.
3. be specific.
4. have its test in the other person.
5. not be an errand.
6. not presuppose any physical or emotional state.
7. not be [emotionally] manipulative
8. have a cap.
9. be in line with the intentions of the playwright" (Bruder, *Practical Handbook* 13–14).

"Actions" used in Coursework or Developed in Classes like this one
to get someone to spill the beans
to get someone to take a chance
to get someone to face the facts
to get someone to crown me king/queen
to get someone to "bite the bullet"
to get someone to "see the silver lining"
to get someone to help me
to get someone to tell me what to do
to get someone to accept my special gift
to get someone to "let me off the hook"
to get someone to "look the other way"
to get someone to see things clearly
to get someone to "buy the bridge"
to get someone to see things my way
to get someone to let go
to get someone to make the right choice
to get someone to accept the truth
to get someone to "buy what I'm selling"
to get someone to "take time to smell the roses"
to get someone to believe in himself/herself
to get someone to "pay the price"
to get someone to see the silliness of the situation
to get someone to tell me what to do*

to get someone to "wake up and smell the coffee"
to get someone to see the seriousness of the situation
to get someone to see the difficulty of the situation
to get someone to show me the way
to show someone who's boss
to get what's owed me
to smack someone into reality
to let someone in on the secret

"Actions" from *A Practical Handbook for the Actor* by Bruder, et al. Page numbers noted parenthetically
"to put someone on the right track" (23)
"to retrieve what is rightfully mine" (30)*
"to beg a loved one for forgiveness" (30)*
"to get someone to tell the truth" (35)
"to prevent a friend from making a terrible mistake" (45)
"to make a loved one 'feel like a million bucks'" (56)

Please add your own new/modified "Actions" on the back of this sheet
*These may cause unwanted focus on oneself.

Some Examples of "Tools" Handout

These cannot be emotions. They are tactics to help you pursue your "action."

"Tools" used in Coursework or Developed in Classes like this one	plead (35)
flatter	level (35)
bribe	threaten (35)
seduce	accuse (35)
barter	Please add new or modified "Tools" here
joke	
reason	
befriend	
lie	
pity	
give the "cold shoulder"	
shock	
touch (if permission given beforehand)	
use "reverse psychology"	
misdirect	
gamble	
ridicule	
"Tools" in *A Practical Handbook For the Actor by* Bruder. Page numbers noted parenthetically	
demand (18)	
cajole (18)	
intimidate (18)	
hear out (23)	
scold (23)	
teach a lesson (23)	
pacify (34)	
explain (34)	
take charge (34)	
promise (34)	
appease (34)	
interrogate (35)	

Name_____

Performance Rubric for Scenes and Monologues

I. Proper Introduction   ____ / 10 points

    ✓Did you introduce yourself using your first and last name?
    ✓Did you say, "This is a scene from the play _____ by the playwright _____, and I will be playing _____?"

II. Memorization   ____ / 20 points

    ✓Did you accurately memorize the text given to you by the playwright?

III. Interpretation/Characterization/Interaction   ____ / 40 points

    ✓Did you follow "Practical Aesthetics," or were you self-focused and/or simply playing a predetermined interpretation of the text?
    ✓Did your performance create a character?
    ✓Was there a relationship between you and your scene partner?

IV. Theatricals   ____ / 20 points

    ✓Did you wear a suitable costume, appropriate attire, or all black?
    ✓Were your set pieces appropriate (if needed)?
    ✓Did you use the appropriate props (if needed)?
    ✓Was your movement appropriate, and did it help you work toward achieving your "action?"

V. Overall Impression   ____ / 10 points

    ✓This may include my reaction, the audience's reaction, and other comments written on the back of this sheet.

Total Score: ____ / 100 points

INDEX

Page numbers in *italic* refer to tables

30 Minute Voice Workout 94, 98, 99

academic standards 42
acting, difficulty 77
acting gurus 1–2
action 68, 71, 74, 76; achieving 79, 94, 108, 117; acting out 70; active pursuit of 84; choice of 13; definition 12; determination 16; essential 58–59; overarching 81, 83; pursuing 104; and speech 94; totality 129
actions handout 59, 139–140
active learning 89
actors, on stage 69–70
Adrian, Barbara 107, 109, 110
American Academy of Otolaryngology 98
American Alliance for Theatre Education 42
Analyzing assigned scenes 46, 64–66, *67*
anticipated questions 34
applause 55, 80
Arizona State University 132
articulation 100, 102–104
Articulation and tongue twisters 100, 102–104, *105*
as if game, the 14, 17, 46, 66, 68–72, 72, *73*, 74, 77, 79–80, 83–84, 96, 130
as ifs 16–17, 60–61, 68, 72, 74, 130, 133
Association for Theatre in Higher Education 1

Atlantic Theatre Acting School 2, 7, 8, 10–11, 18, 19, 54, 59, 75, 87, 88, 107, 108

Baker, George Pierce 132
balance 121
Ballet for Dummies 93
banking model of education 3, 24–27, 35–36, 37, 42, 127–128
Barry, Cecily 108
Barrymore, John 118–119
Bartow, Arthur 7
Bella, Robert 7, 29, 75
Benedetti, Robert 131
Berv, Jason 26–27
Binnicker, Julie 39–40
blocking 81, 121; organic 87
boat/water analogy 17–18
body language 55
body, the, neutral position 92–93, 114, 115
body training: Breathing, stretching, and strengthening 109–112, *113*; Improvisation for movement 121–125, *125–126*; lesson plans 109–126; literature 107; overview 107–108; Presence, Laban kinesphere, and ensemble 114–119, *120*
Bogart, Anne 43, 107, 116, 117, 118
breadth and depth 130–131

Index 145

breath control 89, 96, 98–100, *101*
breath support 107, 109–110, 110–111
Breathing, stretching, and strengthening 109–112, *113*
Brestoff, Richard 7
Brook, Peter 129
Brooks, Jacqueline 40–41
Brooks, Martin 40–41
Bruder, Melissa 7, 12, 57

cap 60–61, 61–62, 74, 76
Carrington, Margaret 119
center 89, 93, 111
challenge 31
chance 9–10
characters: actions 12–13, 16–17, 58–59, 61, 62; as ifs 13–14, 16–17, 60; overarching action 81, 83; wants 12, 58, 61, 62; what they are literally doing 12, 57–58, 61, 62
clarifying questions 34–35
classroom organization 43, 47, 68
class summary 62
class warm-up 57
cognitive trail 43–44
Cohen, Robert 131
Collay, Michelle 22, 29, 30, 38–39, 128
comfort 83
comments 66, 68
communication, non-verbal 55
community 33
competition 132
concentration, breaking 80
constructivism and constructivist approach 3–4, 5, 21–27, 38–39, 127, 133; definition 22–23; as an epistemology 24; instructor as facilitator 24–27; learning theory premises: 26–27; literature 21–23; repetition 11; and understanding 23–24; value 128–129
Constructivist Learning Design 25–26, 29–37, 41, 43, 46; benefits of 30–31; bridge 32–33, 34; elements 30; exhibit 36; groupings 32; pedagogy 30–31; and Praxis 38–39; questions 33–36; reflections 36–37; situation 31–32
constructivist link, the 29, 30
constructivist pedagogy 39, 42, 43, 89, 130; benefits of 30–31; How To's 40–41; lesson planning 39–42
control 49
core: and presence 114–115, 118; strengthening 107, 109–110

Course Calendar 135–136
critical thinking 17, 128–129, 133
cues: verbal 55; visual 14, 55
curricular requirements 42

decisions, clarifying 36
depth 130–131
diaphragm 98
diaphragmatic breathing 89, 94
discipline 8
discussion 69
Dobosiewicz, Troy L.: aims 129–130; career 1–4; introduction to Practical Aesthetics system 2; modified system of Practical Aesthetics 3; pedagogy 3–4; PhD 3
Dubbing 121–122
dynamic encounter 38

education: banking model 3, 24–27, 35–36, 37, 42, 43, 127–128
educational outcomes 42
Educational Theatre Association 42
educational theorists 41
emotional recall 14
emotions 18
engagement 87
ensemble exercises 116–119
Epictetus 8
Examining breath, resonance, and pitch 96, 98–100, *101*
exhibit 36

face, the, role in performance 91–92
facial expressions 91–92
facilitator, instructors as 21, 24–27, 37
feedback, peer to peer 81
films, bridge purposes 33
First day of class introductions 45, 46–47, *48*
focus 11, 29–30; importance 51; on the other person 50, 51, 129, 130; point of 11; situation 31; voice training 91
Fosnot, Catherine Twomey 21, 26–27, 29
freedom to fail 81
Freire, Paulo 3; *Pedagogy of the Oppressed* 24–26, 127–128

Gabler, Ina Clair 22, 39, 128
Gagnon, George W., Jr 22, 29, 30, 38–39, 128
Goddard College, Vermont 2, 6
Green, Maxine 127

groupings 32
guiding questions 34
guru system 1–2

habits 8, 8–9
habituation 9, 21, 30, 39
Hagen, Uta 88, 131
handouts: actions 139–140; Some Examples of Tools 75, 140–141
Hart, Moss 15–18
Howe, Kenneth R. 26–27
humor 124
Hunt, Audrey Jane 96, 98

iceberg metaphor 129
imagination 88–89
improvisation 74, 79, 108; Dubbing 121–122; Japanese Rock Garden 122–123; for movement 121–125, *125–126*; purpose of 121; successful 122; Two Minute Movie 123–124
Improvisation for movement 121–125, *125–126*
impulse training 18
independent learning 128–129
instincts 79, 121
instructors 128; as facilitator 21, 24–27, 37; introducing self 46–47; material 131; role 14, 16, 83, 128–129; stylistic approach 46
integrating questions 35
intensity 17
in the moment 74–75
Itkin. Bella 1–2

James, William 6, 8–9, 9
Japanese Rock Garden 122–123
Jones, Chuck 87, 108, 112, 118–119
journals 45, 104

Kahan, Stanley 131
Kaufman, George S. 15–18
kinesphere 107, 115–119
knowledge 26–27; students 33

Laban, Rudolph 43, 107, 108, 115
Landau, Tina 107, 116, 117, 118
language community 130
Lazarus, Joan 26–27, 131
learner centered practice 26–27
learning 24; constructivist theory 26–27; independent 128–129
Lesson Analysis Blueprint 136–137

Lesson Planning Sheet 137
lesson plans 39: Analyzing assigned scenes 46, 64–66, *67*; body training 109–126; Breathing, stretching, and strengthening 109–112, *113*; First day of class introductions 45, 46–47, *48*; Improvisation for movement 121–125, *125–126*; Level I, II, and III Repetition 46, 53–55, *56*; mind training 45–86; Mind, voice, body, and Level I Repetition 46, 48–51, *52*; narratives 41–42; Playing the 'As if' game 46, 66, 68–72, *73*; Practical Aesthetics scene analysis 46, 57–62, *63*; Praxis 39–43; Presence, Laban kinesphere, and ensemble 114–119, *120*; Rehearsal into Performance 46, 83–85, *85–86*; repetition 48–51, *52*, 53–56, *57*; scene analysis 57–62, *63*, 64–67, *68*, 69–72; Shifting tools 46; stylistic approach 46; templates 39–42; Using tools 46; voice training 90–105
lessons: developmentally appropriate 31–32; links 43–44; order of 43; purpose 31
Level I Repetition 9–10, 48–51, *52*, 53
Level II Repetition 10, 53–54
Level III Repetition 10–11, 54–55
Level I, II, and III Repetition 46, 53–55, *56*
life experience 13
limitations 88
lines: color 76; learning 76–77; memorizing 32
Linklater, Kristin 87, 88, 89, 90
literature 6-7, 21-23, 87, 107
lung capacity 98, 109

Macy, William H. 2, 8, 59
Mamet, David 2, 6, 7, 8–9, 11, 14, 88–89, 127
Mansell, Lilene 87
Marcus, Gabriela 7
Marcus, Paul 7
Marlowe, Bruce 22, 22–23
Maurer, Kelly 107
Mayer, Richard E. 89
meaning, creation of 123
Meek, Julie 40
Meisner, Sanford 9, 17, 57; *Sanford Meisner on Acting* 18–19, 129; technique 18–19
mind training 45, 45–86; aims 45; Analyzing assigned scenes 46, 64–66, *67*; First day of class introductions 45,

46–47, *48*; Level I, II, and III Repetition 46, 53–55, *56*; Mind, voice, body, and Level I Repetition 46, 48–51, *52*; overview 45–46; Playing the 'As if' game 46, 66, 68–72, *73*; Practical Aesthetics scene analysis 46, 57–62, *63*; Rehearsal into Performance 46, 81, 83–85, *85–86*; scenes 45; Shifting tools 46, 77, 79–81, *82*; stylistic approach 46; Using Tools 46, 72, 74–77, *78*
Mind, voice, body, and Level I Repetition 46, 48–51, *52*
mirror exercises 43
mnemonics 47
Monich, Timothy 87
monotone run-through 83
mouth, the, exercising inside 93–94
movement 60, 81, 108; ensemble exercises 116–119; improvisation for 121–125, *125–126*; by instinct 121; lessons 43
muscle coordination 107

National Coalition for Core Arts Standards 42
neutral position 92–93, 114, 115
New York City 2
non-verbal communication 55

observation 18
observation skills. *see* repetition
O'Shaughnessy, Lynn 132
overarching action 81, 83

Page, Marilyn 22, *22–23*
Pass, Susan 21
peer to peer feedback 81
performance 36
Performance Rubric for Scenes and Monologues 141
Perry, Randall Steward 29
personal learning 21
personal space 115–119
Phillips, D. C. 21, 23
physical demands 112
physical imposition 112
physical prowess 109
pitch 99–100
Playing the 'As if' game 46, 66, 68–72, *73*
Positivism 23
practical aesthetics, definition 6
Practical Aesthetics scene analysis 46, 57–62, *63*

Practical Aesthetics system: approach 6; areas of research 131–132; authors introduction to 2; breadth and depth 130–131; comparison with Meisner's technique 18–19; literature 6–7; origins 6; repetition 9–11, 18; scene analysis 11–18; students on 133; use outside acting 132; vocabulary 130
Praxis 4, 38–44; and Constructivist Learning Design 38–39; dynamic encounter 38; lesson planning 39–43; role of 43
presence 107, 112, 114–115, 118–119
Presence, Laban kinesphere, and ensemble 114–119, *120*
processes, integration 130
professionally codified systems 108
pronunciation 102–104
psychological harm 14
purpose 31

questions: anticipated 34; categories 32; clarifying 34–35; guiding 34; importance 35–36; integrating 35
Quinn, Anthony 119

reactions 70–71
readings 11, 119
real-world experience, connecting to 32
reassurance 69
recognition 75
Redding-Jones, Renee 107
reflection 36–37
Rehearsal into Performance 46, 83–85, *85–86*
relaxation 91
repetition 9–11, 18, 71, 72, 76, 77, 130; benefits of 11; Core Exercise 137–138; lesson plans 46, 48–51, *52*, 53–56, *57*; Level I 9–10, 48–51, *52*, 53; Level II 10, 53–54, *56*; Level III 10–11, 54–55, *56*; levels 9, 46; purpose 11
resonance 98–99
respect 47
respectful environment 68
run-throughs, monotone 83

safety 90
Sagor, Richard 44
Sanford Meisner on Acting (Meisner) 18–19, 129
scene analysis 11–18; actions 12–13, 16, 58–59, 61, 62; Analyzing assigned scenes

46, 64–66, *67*; application 15–18; bridge 33; cap 60–61, 61–62; groupings 32; the as if game 14, 17, 46, 66, 68–72, *73*; as ifs 13–14, 16–17, 60–61; instructors role 14, 16; lesson plans 46, 57–62, *63*, 64–67, *68*, 69–72; Playing the 'As if' game 46, 66, 68–72, *73*; Practical Aesthetics scene analysis 46, 57–62, *63*; tactics 15; wants 12, 57–58, 61, 62; what are characters literally doing 12, 57–58, 61, 62; worksheet 57, 59, 76, 138–139
schema 43, 133; accessing 30; construction 23, 30
schema theory 23
schematic links 130
schematic maps 130
Schroeder, Michael 22, 39, 128
scripts 70
self-efficacy 128–129
Shifting tools 46, 77, 79–81, *82*
signposts, visual and aural 123–124
Silverberg, Larry 9, 129
situation 31–32
Skinner, Edith 87, 88, 89, 93, 100, 102–104, 108
Sound of Music Live 132
sources 6–7
spontaneity 108
stage presence 114–115
stage speech 89
stretching 107, 110–112
student misconceptions, identifying 34
students 26, 43; community between 33; knowledge 33; on Practical Aesthetics system 133; self-efficacy 128–129; wants and needs 132
Suzuki exercises 108
system, need for 19

tactics 15
talent 88–89
tasks, open-ended 31
Taylor, Philip 38
templates 39–42
Theatre Educators 19
theatre games 43
theory 4; application 37

tongue twisters 43, 102–103, 103–104
tools 71, 84; definition 72; handout 75, 140–141; repetition 76; shifting 46, 77, 79–81, *82*, 112, 130; uses 75–76, 77; using 46, 72, 74–77, *78*
Toy Story (film) 33–35
truth 23–24, 26–27
Two Minute Movie 123–124

understanding 35–36; constructivism and 23–24
Urcioli, Paul 75, 121, 122
Using tools 46

verbal cues 55
Viewpoints 107, 108, 116, 118
visual cues 14, 55
vocabulary 130, 133
voice register 95
voice training 43: Articulation and tongue twisters 100, 102–104, *105*; breath control 89, 96, 98–100, *101*; Examining breath, resonance, and pitch 96, 98–100, *101*; focus 91; goal 89; inside the mouth 93–94; lesson plans 90–105; literature 87; overview 87–90; pitch 99–100; register 95; resonance 98–99; safety 90; shake it into place 94–95; Warming up the vocal instrument 90–96, **97**; warm-up exercises 89, 90–96, *97*, 104
Vygotsky, Lev 23

Warming up the vocal instrument 90–96, 91, 97
warm-up exercises, voice training 89, 90–96, *97*, 104
Westbrook, Mark 6–7, 14, 15
Wizard of Oz, The (film) 60–62
Word Repetition Game 18
words 129
worksheets 138–139; actions handout 59; scene analysis 57, 59, 76

yoga 108, 110, 111–112
You Can't Take It With You! (Hart and Kaufman) 15–18